"This series is a tremendous resource . understanding of how the gospel is w pastors and scholars doing gospel busii logical feast preparing God's people to a wholly committed to Christ's priorities." ... anu theo-_..uic to all of life with heart and mind

> **BRYAN CHAPELL,** President Emeritus, Covenant Theological Seminary; Senior Pastor, Grace Presbyterian Church, Peoria, Illinois

"Mark Twain may have smiled when he wrote to a friend, 'I didn't have time to write you a short letter, so I wrote you a long letter.' But the truth of Twain's remark remains serious and universal, because well-reasoned, compact writing requires extra time and extra hard work. And this is what we have in the Crossway Bible study series *Knowing the Bible*. The skilled authors and notable editors provide the contours of each book of the Bible as well as the grand theological themes that bind them together as one Book. Here, in a 12-week format, are carefully wrought studies that will ignite the mind and the heart."

> **R. KENT HUGHES,** Visiting Professor of Practical Theology, Westminster Theological Seminary

"*Knowing the Bible* brings together a gifted team of Bible teachers to produce a high-quality series of study guides. The coordinated focus of these materials is unique: biblical content, provocative questions, systematic theology, practical application, and the gospel story of God's grace presented all the way through Scripture."

> **PHILIP G. RYKEN,** President, Wheaton College

"These *Knowing the Bible* volumes provide a significant and very welcome variation on the general run of inductive Bible studies. This series provides substantial instruction, as well as teaching through the very questions that are asked. *Knowing the Bible* then goes even further by showing how any given text links with the gospel, the whole Bible, and the formation of theology. I heartily endorse this orientation of individual books to the whole Bible and the gospel, and I applaud the demonstration that sound theology was not something invented later by Christians, but is right there in the pages of Scripture."

> **GRAEME L. GOLDSWORTHY,** former lecturer, Moore Theological College; author, *According to Plan, Gospel and Kingdom, The Gospel in Revelation,* and *Gospel and Wisdom*

"What a gift to earnest, Bible-loving, Bible-searching believers! The organization and structure of the Bible study format presented through the *Knowing the Bible* series is so well conceived. Students of the Word are led to understand the content of passages through perceptive, guided questions, and they are given rich insights and application all along the way in the brief but illuminating sections that conclude each study. What potential growth in depth and breadth of understanding these studies offer! One can only pray that vast numbers of believers will discover more of God and the beauty of his Word through these rich studies."

> **BRUCE A. WARE,** Professor of Christian Theology, The Southern Baptist Theological Seminary

KNOWING THE BIBLE

J. I. Packer, Theological Editor
Dane C. Ortlund, Series Editor
Lane T. Dennis, Executive Editor

• • • • • •

Genesis	Ecclesiastes	John	Colossians/
Exodus	Isaiah	Acts	Philemon
Leviticus	Jeremiah	Romans	Hebrews
Joshua	Daniel	1 Corinthians	James
Ruth, Esther	Hosea	2 Corinthians	Revelation
Ezra, Nehemiah	Matthew	Galatians	
Psalms	Mark	Ephesians	
Proverbs	Luke	Philippians	

• • • • • •

J. I. PACKER is Board of Governors' Professor of Theology at Regent College (Vancouver, BC). Dr. Packer earned his DPhil at the University of Oxford. He is known and loved worldwide as the author of the best-selling book *Knowing God*, as well as many other titles on theology and the Christian life. He serves as the General Editor of the ESV Bible and as the Theological Editor for the *ESV Study Bible*.

LANE T. DENNIS is President of Crossway, a not-for-profit publishing ministry. Dr. Dennis earned his PhD from Northwestern University. He is Chair of the ESV Bible Translation Oversight Committee and Executive Editor of the *ESV Study Bible*.

DANE C. ORTLUND is Executive Vice President of Bible Publishing and Bible Publisher at Crossway. He is a graduate of Covenant Theological Seminary (MDiv, ThM) and Wheaton College (BA, PhD). Dr. Ortlund has authored several books and scholarly articles in the areas of Bible, theology, and Christian living.

HOSEA

A 12-WEEK STUDY

Lydia Brownback

CROSSWAY®

WHEATON, ILLINOIS

Crossway is a publishing ministry of Good News Publishers.

VP		26	25	24	23	22	21	20	19	18	17	16
15	14	13	12	11	10	9	8	7	6	5	4	3	2	1

TABLE OF CONTENTS

▲

SERIES PREFACE

KNOWING THE BIBLE, as the series title indicates, was created to help readers know and understand the meaning, the message, and the God of the Bible. Each volume in the series consists of 12 units that progressively take the reader through a clear, concise study of that book of the Bible. In this way, any given volume can fruitfully be used in a 12-week format either in group study, such as in a church-based context, or in individual study. Of course, these 12 studies could be completed in fewer or more than 12 weeks, as convenient, depending on the context in which they are used.

Each study unit gives an overview of the text at hand before digging into it with a series of questions for reflection or discussion. The unit then concludes by highlighting the gospel of grace in each passage ("Gospel Glimpses"), identifying whole-Bible themes that occur in the passage ("Whole-Bible Connections"), and pinpointing Christian doctrines that are affirmed in the passage ("Theological Soundings").

The final component to each unit is a section for reflecting on personal and practical implications from the passage at hand. The layout provides space for recording responses to the questions proposed, and we think readers need to do this to get the full benefit of the exercise. The series also includes definitions of key words. These definitions are indicated by a note number in the text and are found at the end of each chapter.

Lastly, for help in understanding the Bible in this deeper way, we would urge the reader to use the ESV Bible and the *ESV Study Bible*, which are available online at www.esvbible.org. The *Knowing the Bible* series is also available online. Additional 12-week studies covering each book of the Bible will be added as they become available.

May the Lord greatly bless your study as you seek to know him through knowing his Word.

J. I. Packer
Lane T. Dennis

Week 1: Overview

Getting Acquainted

Hosea is primarily a love story, specifically one of redemptive love. The pain Hosea has endured in his marriage to unfaithful Gomer uniquely qualifies him for his prophetic ministry to the Lord's unfaithful people. Failing to trust the Lord, Israel has sought security in foreign powers and false gods. Yet, as Hosea is eager to show, Israel's unfaithfulness has not diminished God's love for them. Hosea paints Israel's spiritual adultery with vivid images, calling God's people with both warnings and heartfelt appeals to turn back to the Lord. Failure to repent will result in punishment, but God takes no delight in that prospect. Rather, he desires them to turn from idols to him, their true husband and the only one who can provide for their needs.

The book, primarily poetry, is dominated by oracles of judgment. The first three chapters are autobiographical, recounting how Hosea responded to the unfaithfulness of his wife, Gomer, redeeming her from the slavery into which her unfaithfulness had led. In the remainder of the book, chapters 4–14, Hosea uses his experience as a parable[1] to depict the Lord's broken relationship with his covenant people and his intention to redeem them from their enslavement to sin. (For further background, see the *ESV Study Bible*, pages 1619–1622; available online at www.esvbible.org.)

Placing It in the Larger Story

Hosea prophesied during a dark time in Israel's history. Worship of the Lord had been abandoned in favor of idol worship, which led to exile from the Promised Land. But in God's plan, exile became the means to eventual restoration. The book of Hosea shows the wickedness and folly of idol worship and points by contrast to the one true God, who not only can provide all that his people need but is willing to do so despite their rejection of him. Both Hosea's personal story and the overall historical context to which it points demonstrate God's way of salvation in Christ. God stands ready to forgive and restore those who turn to him, and he has provided the ransom[2] from slavery through Jesus Christ. The marriage theme in Hosea finds its fullest expression in Christ's love for the church (Eph. 5:25–27).

Key Verse

"I will heal their apostasy; I will love them freely, for my anger has turned from them" (Hos. 14:4).

Date and Historical Background

Hosea, one of the Old Testament's 12 "minor prophets," ministered during the latter half of the eighth century BC, prophesying primarily to Ephraim (the northern kingdom of Israel) in the decades leading up to the fall of Samaria to the Assyrian Empire. Israel's kingship had grown increasingly ineffective, while foreign powers, particularly Assyria, had grown in power and become a dominant threat. Worship of Baal, the weather and fertility god worshiped in Syria-Palestine, was rampant and involved God's people in open immorality at pagan shrines. Failure to repent of this apostasy resulted in Israel's downfall and captivity in 722 BC.

Outline

I. Biography: Hosea's Family (1:1–3:5)

   A. Introduction (1:1)

   B. Command to marry (1:2)

   C. Birth of children (1:3–9)

   D. Covenant renewal at Jezreel (1:10–11)

   E. Legal proceedings against the wayward wife (2:1–13)

F. Covenant relationship reestablished (2:14–23)

G. Command to remarry, with the expectation of a king like David (3:1–5)

II. Hosea Spells Out His Parable with Accusations, Warnings, and Promises (4:1–14:9)

A. Legal proceedings continued (4:1–19)

B. Adultery in high places (5:1–14)

C. Appeal: return and be raised (5:15–6:3)

D. Transgressors of the covenant (6:4–7:3)

E. Four similes for unfaithful Israel: oven, cake, dove, treacherous bow (7:4–16)

F. Israel's hypocrisy (8:1–14)

G. Warnings: no worship in a foreign land (9:1–9)

H. More similes for unfaithful Israel: grapes, vine, calf, toddler (9:10–11:11)

I. Dependence on alliances (11:12–12:1)

J. Further indictment based on historical review (12:2–14)

K. Worship of man-made gods (13:1–8)

L. Rejecting the only hope they have (13:9–16)

M. Closing appeals (14:1–9)

As You Get Started

What is your understanding of how Hosea advances the storyline of the Bible?

How does this book clarify our understanding of God's love for us in Christ?

How does Hosea deepen our understanding of the nature and spiritual danger of idol worship?

As You Finish This Unit . . .

Take a few minutes as you begin this study of Hosea to ask God to humble your heart and open your eyes to comprehend more fully both the depth of your sinfulness and the extent of God's redeeming love for you.

Definitions

[1] **Parable** – A story that uses everyday imagery and activities to communicate a spiritual truth. Jesus often taught in parables (e.g., Matthew 13).

[2] **Ransom** – A price paid to redeem, or buy back, someone who had become enslaved or something that had been lost to someone else. Jesus described his ministry as serving others and giving his life as a ransom for many (Mark 10:45).

WEEK 2: HOSEA'S FAMILY

Hosea 1:1–3:5

▲

In this first section, God instructs Hosea to marry Gomer, a woman who will prove to be unfaithful to him (Hos. 1:2). Hosea's marriage is meant to serve as a vivid illustration of the broken covenant[1] between the Lord and Israel, as do the names of the three children Gomer bears (1:4, 6, 9), two of whom are not fathered by Hosea. The prophet then builds a legal case against his adulterous wife, which points to how God will deal with his adulterous people (2:1–23). God then instructs the prophet to go and reclaim his wife and bring her home (3:1–5), which foreshadows what God has planned for his people. Although Israel has forsaken the Lord, God will remain faithful to his covenant and restore his people to himself.

The Big Picture

Hosea 1:1–3:5 shows God's heart toward his people as that of a husband toward his beloved and likens Israel to an unfaithful spouse.

> ## Reflection and Discussion

Read through the complete passage for this study, Hosea 1:1–3:5. Then review the questions below and write notes concerning this introductory section. (For further background, see the *ESV Study Bible*, pages 1623–1627; available online at www .esvbible.org.)

1. Hosea's Wife and Children (1:1–8)

God instructs Hosea to marry Gomer, who will prove to be an unfaithful wife (Hos. 1:2). Hosea's broken marriage will reflect Israel's unfaithfulness to God. What does God's instruction reveal about the nature of his covenant with Israel? (See also Ex. 6:6–8; Ezek. 16:8–14.)

"He went and took Gomer, the daughter of Diblaim, and she conceived and bore him a son" (Hos. 1:3). Hosea was told by God to name his firstborn son "Jezreel" (v. 4), which points back to the wicked Israelite king Ahab, who murdered Naboth, a godly man from Jezreel (see 1 Kings 21). Ahab's primary evil was to promote worship of Baal as the national religion of Israel. How do the naming of Hosea's child and the story from 1 Kings 21 reveal the nature of Israel's current unfaithfulness?

"She conceived again and bore a daughter. . . . she conceived and bore a son" (Hos. 1:6, 8). The wording used to describe the birth of Gomer's second and third children suggests that Hosea was not their father, which is reinforced by the names given to the children: "No Mercy" and "Not My People." What do these names reveal about what Israel stands to lose because of her unfaithfulness to the Lord?

"Yet the number of the children of Israel shall be like the sand of the sea, which cannot be measured or numbered" (Hos. 1:10). Hosea echoes the promise God made long ago to Abraham (Gen. 22:17; 32:12), a promise God would keep despite Israel's ongoing disobedience. What do the things promised in Hosea 1:10–11 reveal about the nature of salvation?

2. Israel's Unfaithfulness Punished (2:1–13)

"Plead with your mother, plead . . . that she put away her whoring from her face" (Hos. 2:2). As if speaking to his illegitimate children, Hosea speaks God's words to Israel, clarifying where their unfaithfulness is taking them and what will happen if they refuse to repent. Why is this worded as a plea?

The nature and results of idolatry are uncovered in this section, first in the words of Gomer/Israel (2:5) and then in God's response (2:6–13). Based on this passage, how do idols deceive their worshipers, and how does God's judgment increase in intensity when idolaters refuse to repent? Where do we see these patterns in our culture and our own lives?

"I will hedge up her way with thorns" (Hos. 2:6). Israel is determined to pursue her lovers (v. 5), but God will prevent her from succeeding. As a jealous husband who has been wronged by the infidelity of his people, he desires them to come to their senses and return to him. How are his actions here—hedging with thorns, building a wall, obscuring Israel's idolatrous paths—actually merciful? What does this reveal about the nature of godly jealousy?

God will destroy the vines and fig trees, which Israel has attributed to Baal (Hos. 2:12). Unlike the salvation the Lord holds forth—an unearned gift of grace—idols always exact wages from their worshipers. In their unbridled pursuit of Baal, God's people have forgotten him (v. 13; see also Jer. 3:21; 18:15). Review the warnings Moses gave to Israel before they entered the Promised Land: Deuteronomy 5:15; 8:2–3, 18; 15:15; 16:3, 12; 24:18. Based on his warnings, what specifically have the people forgotten?

3. The Lord's Mercy on Israel (2:14–23)

Although God will punish Israel for covenant unfaithfulness, his intention is restorative, not destructive, which is made clear in 2:14–15. What characteristics of God's love are seen in this passage, and how is such a love conducive to repentance? (See also Rom. 2:4.)

"In that day, declares the LORD, you will call me 'My Husband'" (Hos. 2:16). The remainder of Hosea 2 presents a description of what life will be like when the marriage between God and his people is restored. Through a series of "I will" statements, God paints an enticing picture to woo Israel. How is the nature of true repentance, meaning "to turn around," reflected in the promises God makes in these statements?

4. Hosea Redeems His Wife (3:1–5)

God commands Hosea to redeem his wife and bring her home. The fact that Hosea has to purchase Gomer shows the desperate situation into which her adultery has brought her. In like manner, God will redeem his unfaithful people, after which they will undergo a forced separation from all that has fueled their idol worship. What effect will this forced separation have upon God's people, and what outcome does he intend?

Read through the following three sections on *Gospel Glimpses*, *Whole-Bible Connections*, and *Theological Soundings*. Then take time to consider the *Personal Implications* these sections may have for you.

Gospel Glimpses

DIVINE HEDGE. By erecting barriers along the path of sin, God frustrates the efforts of Israel to run from him. In mercy God will not give his people up to their sinful desires (Rom. 1:18–25) but will intervene to keep them from destruction. Divine hedges are specific and personal, as the psalmist notes in wonder: "You hem me in, behind and before, and lay your hand upon me. Such knowledge is too wonderful for me" (Ps. 139:5–6).

TENDERNESS. Adulterous Israel deserves to be cut off in anger from God's love; they have broken the heart of their divine husband. Yet far from the typical response of a wronged husband, God woos his people with terms of endearment. This tenderness is reflected in Jesus, who spoke with compassion to guilty sinners and gently wooed them to embrace life in him.

BETROTH. The old covenant God established with his people was designed to reflect the love, fidelity, and exclusivity of marriage. This finds its fulfillment in the new covenant in Christ, the husband of his bride, the church. He "loved the church and gave himself up for her" and "nourishes and cherishes" his bride (Eph. 5:25–28).

Whole-Bible Connections

NAMING. As instructed by the Lord, Hosea gives Gomer's children prophetic names (Hos. 1:4, 6, 8). The names are meant to serve as symbols of covenant breaking and coming judgment. Isaiah also used naming prophetically (Isa. 7:3; 8:1–3, 18). In the Old Testament, naming was authoritative. At creation God instructed Adam to name the animals, signifying man's dominion over all creatures as God's vice-regent (Gen. 1:26; 2:19–20). Additionally, the name given to a child, or the renaming of an adult, often pointed to some distinguishing characteristic or epoch in the life of the one being named (see, e.g., Gen. 17:4–5; 32:28). Names were also signs, most especially in Isaiah's prophecy of the Messiah: "The Lord himself will give you a sign. Behold, the virgin shall conceive and bear a son, and shall call his name Immanuel" (Isa. 7:14), the significance of which is made clear at the birth of the Messiah (Matt. 1:20–23).

WHOREDOM. "Go, take to yourself a wife of whoredom and have children of whoredom, for the land commits great whoredom by forsaking the LORD" (Hos. 1:2). Whoredom in the Old Testament is typically linked to idolatry, a common temptation that took hold after God's people entered the Promised Land; the people did not obey God's instructions to destroy the idols and idol worshipers who dwelt there (see Ps. 106:34–39). Idol worship frequently involved illicit sexual practices, and participating in such practices, involving both heart and body, constituted unfaithfulness to the Lord and covenant breaking. The whoredom of idolatry is described in the prophets with much pathos and often with graphic sexual imagery (see Jer. 2:20–24; 3:1–2; Ezekiel 16; 23).

KING DAVID. "Afterward the children of Israel shall return and seek the LORD their God, and David their king, and they shall come in fear to the LORD and to his goodness in the latter days" (Hos. 3:5). Hosea's prophecy of future restoration to the Davidic kingship signifies that God's people—both Judah and the northern kingdom—will one day be reunited under one headship, which at the time of Hosea's prophecy had not been the case for two centuries. Hosea's words find ultimate fulfillment in the Messiah, who will come from the royal line of David and will bring all things together under his divine kingship.

Theological Soundings

SIN AS IDOLATRY. Hosea's primary message is a call away from idolatry, specifically the worship of Baal. Israel's history is a cycle of failing to trust the Lord and of turning instead to idols to meet their needs. Idolatry is foolish and destructive because there is only one God; trusting in anything besides him robs him of the devotion and glory he alone deserves. Idols in the Old Testament consisted primarily of the nature and fertility deities worshiped by surrounding nations. However, anything that displaces trust in and allegiance to God becomes an idol. According to Jesus, money can become an idol (Matt. 6:24). As is made so clear in the Old Testament prophets, lust and impurity often accompany idolatry (Eph. 5:5; Col. 3:5), as do demons[2] (1 Cor. 10:19–20).

PURIFICATION. When Hosea retrieves Gomer and brings her home, he segregates her from all that had drawn her away (Hos. 3:3). The separation will result in a restoration of marital purity. The greater application of Hosea's command to Gomer is the purification of God's people, which will occur when they are separated through exile from everything that has fueled their spiritual adultery: "The children of Israel shall dwell many days without king or prince, without sacrifice or pillar, without ephod or household gods" (v. 4). But God's purification process, while painful, is designed to be restorative and will result ultimately in blessing for his people in every era.

Personal Implications

Take time to reflect on the implications of Hosea 1:1–3:5 for your own life today. Consider what you have learned that might point to idols in your life and the need to return to your divine husband. Make notes below on the personal implications for your walk with the Lord of the (1) *Gospel Glimpses*, (2) *Whole-Bible Connections*, (3) *Theological Soundings*, and (4) this passage as a whole.

1. Gospel Glimpses

2. Whole-Bible Connections

3. Theological Soundings

4. Hosea 1:1–3:5

As You Finish This Unit . . .

Take a moment now to ask for the Lord's blessing and help as you continue in this study of Hosea. Look back through this unit of study and reflect on some key things the Lord may be teaching you.

Definitions

[1] **Covenant** – A binding agreement between two parties, typically involving a formal statement of their relationship, a list of stipulations and obligations for both parties, a list of witnesses to the agreement, and a list of curses for unfaithfulness and blessings for faithfulness to the agreement. The OT is more properly understood as the old covenant, meaning the agreement established between God and his people prior to the coming of Jesus Christ and the establishment of the new covenant (NT).

[2] **Demon** – An evil spirit that can inhabit a human being and influence him or her to carry out its will. Demons are fallen angels. They were created by God and are always limited by God. Jesus and his followers cast out many demons, demonstrating Jesus' superiority over them. All demons will one day be destroyed, along with Satan (Matt. 25:41; Rev. 20:10).

WEEK 3: LEGAL PROCEEDINGS

Hosea 4:1–19

▲

The Place of the Passage

Now that Hosea has set forth Israel's unfaithfulness to God through his vivid personal illustration, he elaborates on all that the Lord has against his people. This section of the prophecy is like a prosecutor making a case in court, detailing specific charges and the corresponding penalties that await. All Israel is addressed, but the priests are called out specifically for their failure. The primary charge is turning from God to idols, specifically Baal.

The Big Picture

In Hosea 4:1–19, specific aspects of Baal worship are illuminated, and so is the inevitable destruction that will follow a failure to repent.

> ## Reflection and Discussion

Read through the entire text for this study, Hosea 4:1–19. Then interact with the following questions and record your notes on them. (For further background, see the *ESV Study Bible*, pages 1627–1629.)

1. No Knowledge (4:1–3)

As the Lord lays out his case against Israel, he accuses the people of having no faithfulness, steadfast love, or knowledge of him (4:1). Failure to be faithful and to love fit well with the marriage metaphor in Hosea, but a lack of knowledge might at first seem surprising here. Nevertheless, it is a key idea in the book. What does this section overall reveal about the nature of this missing knowledge?

In place of faithfulness, love, and knowledge are all manner of sins (4:2). God's commandments have been willfully broken, and the whole creation suffers as a result (v. 3)—as it has ever since the fall[1] (see Gen. 3:17–18; Rom. 8:22). What does this indicate about the nature of sin?

2. Accusation against the Priests (4:4–9)

God narrows his focus from the people in general to the priests, who were responsible for teaching the people God's law and therefore bore a greater responsibility for the current apostasy. For what does God hold them accountable? The judgment for their failure will be rejection by God—rejection not only of the priests but also of the priests' children. How does Exodus 29:44–46 reveal the significance of this consequence?

Prosperity has fostered a spirit of independence from the Lord, which has made the people callous to sin, and it will cost them their glorious heritage (Hos. 4:7). This is not the first time in Israel's history that priests have abused their office (see 1 Sam. 2:27–36), nor would it be the last. Much later, long after the Jews had returned from exile, the priests again failed to carry out their high calling. Read Malachi 2:1–9. What similarities do you see between the actions of the priests here in Hosea and those of Malachi's day? The repetitive failure of the temple priests points to the need for a priest who would keep God's covenant and feed God's Word to God's people, and such a priest is found only in Christ, who fulfilled all priestly obligations (see Heb. 5:1–10).

The priests are guilty also because "they feed on the sin of my people" (Hos. 4:8). The sin here might be in reference to the burnt sacrifice the priests were required to offer on behalf of the people and which they were then entitled to eat (see Lev. 6:25–30). Far from carrying out their calling to provide atonement for sin, the priests have become greedy, and their privileged position will not shield them from God's judgment (Hos. 4:9). Why do you think greed is a fitting description for those in pursuit of sin?

3. The Path of Idolatry (4:10–14)

The nature and outcome of idol worship are revealed clearly in this section, and one of the consequences shown is futility: "They shall eat, but not be satisfied" (4:10; see also Mic. 6:14; Hag. 1:6). The book of Ecclesiastes also emphasizes the general futility that resulted from the fall. How does Romans 8:18–21 uncover the grace of God that reverses this consequence?

Idols never deliver what they promise. God's people had come to believe that the worship of Baal would result in increased fertility and agricultural fruitfulness, and their worship practices involving ritual sexuality mirrored this belief. According to Hosea 4:11, what led Israel to "cherish" these ritual practices and forsake the Lord?

A link is made in this section between alcohol abuse and sexual immorality, both of which can be aspects of an idolatrous heart. According to Hosea 4:11, what danger is posed by these two sins? How does Ephesians 4:17–19 echo this passage in Hosea, and what insight does it add to it?

The futility of idol worship is emphasized again in Hosea 4:12: "My people inquire of a piece of wood." Worshiping idols is not only futile; it is ludicrous. How do Psalm 115:4–8 and Isaiah 44:9–20 further illuminate not only the folly of worshiping idols but also the destructive power of doing so?

Why does idolatry have intergenerational consequences? How is this depicted in Hosea 4:13–14?

4. Wrapped in the Wings of Idols (4:15–19)

Judah, the southern kingdom, is warned to stay away from Israel in order to avoid following Israel's downward path. Specifically, Judah is to avoid the shrines in Gilgal and Beth Aven (4:15). Those two shrines had been set up in the north for the worship of the Lord but were a violation of God's command that he be worshiped in one central place, which was located in the south. Read Deuteronomy 12:8–14 and 1 Kings 12:25–33. What do these passages reveal about worship that pleases God and about the temptations that work against that?

Israel, called "Ephraim" in Hosea 4:17, has become enslaved, wrapped in the wind (or spirit) of idols (v. 19). Twice in verses 17–19, shame is noted as the inevitable result. Based on God's overall indictment of his people in Hosea 4, how specifically will this shame be manifested?

Read through the following three sections on *Gospel Glimpses*, *Whole-Bible Connections*, and *Theological Soundings*. Then take time to consider the *Personal Implications* these sections may have for you.

Gospel Glimpses

GREAT HIGH PRIEST. The priests in Hosea's day were to teach God's law and offer right sacrifices on behalf of God's people, but they failed miserably. This sacred office, however, was established to demonstrate the need for a mediator,[2] one who would fulfill all the priestly requirements contained in the law, and this was provided in Jesus Christ, our Great High Priest, who was "holy, innocent, unstained, separated from sinners, and exalted above the heavens," and whose sacrifice of himself sufficed once for all (Heb. 7:23–28).

SATISFACTION. God is faithful to expose idols as false gods and the worship of them as futile. The inevitable destructive consequences of idolatry point us to the only source of true satisfaction, God himself. Unlike idols that "take away the understanding" (Hos. 4:10) and bring shame (vv. 18–19), Christ came in order that we "may have life and have it abundantly" (John 10:10).

Whole-Bible Connections

THE LAND. "The land mourns, and all who dwell in it languish" (Hos. 4:3). The effect of sin on all of creation is seen from the time of the fall, when the ground was cursed because of Adam (Gen. 3:17–19). The prophets speak of the earth's mourning (Isa. 24:4; Jer. 4:28; Joel 1:10), as does the apostle Paul in the New Testament (Rom. 8:19–22). Yet at the consummation[3] the effects of the fall will be reversed, and creation will be "set free from its bondage to corruption" (Rom. 8:21; see also Isa. 11:6–9). On the last day all of creation will become beautiful, productive, and easy to live in.

PRIESTHOOD. Under the old covenant system, priests were set apart to teach God's law and to offer right sacrifices on behalf of God's people, but they failed miserably from the time of Aaron, who led the people in false worship of the golden calf (Exodus 32). Throughout the Old Testament we are shown the corruption of the priests as a significant factor in the nation's downfall. This sacred office, however, was established for the purpose of pointing God's people to their need for a better priest, one who would fulfill all the priestly requirements contained in the law, and this was provided in Jesus Christ. Following Christ's perfect and complete sacrifice, there was no more need for the Levitical priesthood. In its place is the priesthood of believers, who are "being built up as a spiritual house, to be a holy priesthood, to offer spiritual sacrifices acceptable to God through Jesus Christ" (1 Pet. 2:5; see also v. 9).

Theological Soundings

KNOWLEDGE OF GOD. God condescends to make himself known to human beings, and he has always done so, most fully and finally in the person of his Son. Although the people of Hosea's day lacked that full and final revelation, they had the covenant, the prophetic word, and all else they needed to know God (see Rom. 1:19–20). Their failure to know God was due to their rejection of revelation (Hos. 4:6). How much more are we without excuse: "Long ago, at many times and in many ways, God spoke to our fathers by the prophets, but in these last days he has spoken to us by his Son" (Heb. 1:1–2). While Jesus walked this earth, he revealed the "radiance of the glory of God and the exact imprint of his nature" (Heb. 1:3), yet the majority of mankind rejected this knowledge, to their own destruction. Yet the privilege stands: we are able to know God fully, because Jesus has made him known (John 1:18).

SIN AS DOWNWARD SPIRAL. Unrepentant sin leads inevitably to more sin, to the point where all bounds are broken and bloodshed follows bloodshed (Hos. 4:2). Unchecked sin leads to increased desire for it (v. 8), which is enslavement of the worst kind (vv. 10, 19), and eventually to utter shame (vv. 7, 18–19) and judgment (vv. 9, 14). Increased desire for sin is the beginning of God's judgment on the sinner: "Since they did not see fit to acknowledge God, God gave them up to a debased mind to do what ought not to be done" (Rom. 1:28). Yet grace is inherent in this "giving over." As the restraint on sin is lifted, the resulting misery is designed to humble the hardened who cry out for God's mercy, which he is always ready to shower on truly repentant hearts.

THE HARDENING EFFECT OF PROSPERITY. "The more they increased, the more they sinned against me" (Hos. 4:7). Prosperity easily breeds a spirit of independence from God, something that occurred repeatedly once God's people entered the Promised Land. Deprivation, whether perceived or real, can be a divine blessing, as it serves to remind God's people that he is their true provider (see Deut. 8:1–3). The false sense of autonomy often accompanying prosperity lies at the root of the love of money (1 Tim. 6:10). Jesus proved this truth in his encounter with a rich young man, who chose his wealth over riches in God's kingdom, leading Jesus to say, "It is easier for a camel to go through the eye of a needle than for a rich man to enter the kingdom of God" (Matt. 19:16–24).

▶ Personal Implications

Take time to reflect on the implications of Hosea 4:1–19 for your own life today. Consider what you have learned that might lead you to trust more fully in God's gracious promises. Make notes below on the personal implications for your walk with the Lord of the (1) *Gospel Glimpses*, (2) *Whole-Bible Connections*, (3) *Theological Soundings*, and (4) this passage as a whole.

1. Gospel Glimpses

----

2. Whole-Bible Connections

----

3. Theological Soundings

_____

_____

_____

_____

_____

_____

4. Hosea 4:1–19

_____

_____

_____

_____

_____

_____

As You Finish This Unit . . .

Take a moment now to ask for the Lord's blessing and help as you continue in this study of Hosea. Then look back through this unit to reflect on key things the Lord may be teaching you.

Definitions

[1] **Fall, the** – Adam and Eve's disobedience of God by eating the fruit from the tree of the knowledge of good and evil, resulting in their loss of innocence and favor with God and the introduction of sin and its effects into the world (Genesis 3; Rom. 5:12–21; 1 Cor. 15:21–22).

[2] **Mediator** – One who intercedes between parties to resolve a conflict or achieve a goal. Jesus is the mediator between God and rebellious humanity (1 Tim. 2:5; compare Heb. 9:15; 12:24).

[3] **Consummation** – In Christian theology, the final and full establishment of the kingdom of God, when the heavens and earth will be made new and God will rule over all things forever (2 Pet. 3:13; Revelation 11; 19–22).

WEEK 4: PUNISHMENT COMING

Hosea 5:1–6:3

▲

The Place of the Passage

The Lord's indictment continues, especially against the rulers who have led God's people into unfaithfulness. Because they refuse to acknowledge their transgressions, the Lord will come in fury and make his people waste away. Nevertheless, God desires his people to return to him and thereby avoid the coming judgment.

The Big Picture

Hosea 5:1–6:3 shows us that while God is patient, unrepentant sin will eventually lead to judgment.

> ### Reflection and Discussion

Read through the complete passage for this study, Hosea 5:1–6:3. Then review the questions below and write your notes on them. (For further background, see the *ESV Study Bible*, pages 1629–1631.)

1. Adultery in High Places (5:1–14)

Hosea calls Israel's leaders, both priests and kings, to account for their guilt because they have become a "snare at Mizpah" and a "net spread upon Tabor" (5:1). The reference to Mizpah and Tabor points back to a better time in Israel's history. What do the images of "snare" and "net" seem to imply? How does the wisdom contained in Proverbs 1:17–19 add to the picture here in Hosea?

"The revolters have gone deep into slaughter" (Hos. 5:2). This is likely a reference to the child sacrifice of Baal worship. If so, it sheds light on how the leaders in Israel have promoted Baal. How is this likelihood reinforced by Psalm 106:36–38? According to the psalm, what underlies and fuels this horrific ritual?

Although Israel has failed to know the Lord, the Lord knows Israel. God sees that the people have become utterly defiled through idol worship and that "their deeds do not permit them to return to their God" (Hos. 5:4). Why do their deeds block the way back to God, and what does this reveal about the nature of idolatry?

Both Israel and Judah "shall stumble" in guilt (5:5), but this stumbling is no mere misstep. How do Isaiah 8:11–15 and 1 Peter 2:6–8 bring forth its ultimate meaning?

Because God's people offer him worship only in pretense, they will not find him (Hos. 5:6). The ordinances God appointed for worship were meant to deepen the people's devotion to him, but now the people practice them as a way of manipulating God. They have no qualms about mixing elements of Canaanite religion into their worship. How does Isaiah 1:11–15 shed light on why God has withdrawn from them?

A specific accusation against Judah's leadership is that they "have become like those who move the landmark" (Hos. 5:10), which involved laying claim to land rightfully belonging to another (see Deut. 19:14; 27:17). After God brought his people into Canaan, he apportioned the land in a detailed way among the tribes of Israel (Joshua 13–21). In light of this history, why was land-grabbing so abhorrent in God's sight?

"Ephraim is oppressed, crushed in judgment, because he was determined to go after filth" (Hos. 5:11). "Filth" here can be translated also as "human precepts." What renders human precepts analogous to filth? How would you define the human precepts of Hosea's day that the people were "determined" to pursue? How about those of our day?

God has become "like a moth" to Ephraim and "like dry rot" to Judah (5:12). What do these images convey, and how does that imagery speak to God's faithfulness in exposing the impotence of idols? The imagery changes in verse 14, where God likens himself to a lion. How is this image different, and what is its import here?

----

2. The Lord's Appeal (5:15–6:3)

God will tear and strike down his people (Hos. 6:1), but rather than driving them farther from him, the punishment will bring healing and restore them to a right knowledge of God. How is this expressed in 6:3? What does this teach us about God and his ways?

"After two days he will revive us; on the third day he will raise us up, that we may live before him" (Hos. 6:2). How do Hosea's words here point to what underlies all repentance and the restoration of God's people? How does Luke 24:44–47 reveal this truth?

Read through the following three sections on *Gospel Glimpses*, *Whole-Bible Connections*, and *Theological Soundings*. Then take time to consider the *Personal Implications* these sections may have for you.

Gospel Glimpses

DISCIPLINE. "I will discipline all of them" (Hos. 5:2). Rather than destroy his wayward people as they deserve, God disciplines them as a sign of fatherly love and favor (Prov. 3:11–12) intended to bring about repentance (Hos. 5:15–6:3; see also Ps. 119:67) and spiritual growth (Heb. 12:5–11). The glimpses of divine fatherhood here point to the work of Christ, through whom believers are adopted as God's sons (Rom. 8:15).

RAISED.[1] "On the third day he will raise us up" (Hos. 6:2). The Lord would bring down his people in judgment for their sin, but following the painful discipline they would return to the Lord with renewed zeal. Hosea's prophetic words are mirrored in the experience of Jonah, who was "raised" from the depths of the seas on the third day (Jonah 1:17). These third-day references point forward to Christ, who, after suffering and dying on behalf of God's people, was raised from death on the third day (Matt. 12:40; 1 Cor. 15:4).

Whole-Bible Connections

INHERITANCE. God's wrath stands upon the "princes of Judah" because they have become like "those who move the landmark" (Hos. 5:10). God's law upheld property rights, which reflects God's intention for his people to enjoy his temporal gifts, each of which is governed in detail by the divine giver. We see this in the book of Joshua, where particular lots of the Promised Land are apportioned to various clans (Joshua 13–21). In the New Testament, the inheritance God gives, which is also to be cherished and guarded, is spiritual rather than temporal (Eph. 1:11–14; Col. 1:11–12; Heb. 9:15; 1 Pet. 1:3–5).

SIN AS SICKNESS. In the Old Testament Prophets, sickness and injury serve often as a visible outworking of an invisible malady. Hosea indicates that Israel "saw his sickness, and Judah his wound," but in their case it served only to exacerbate their pursuit of idols (Hos. 5:13). The analogy of sin to sickness finds its fullest expression in the life of Jesus, who healed numerous individuals to point to his overarching purpose—healing sinners of their sin. While we usually cannot make a certain connection between an individual's physical ailment and sin, the fact remains that all sickness is a result of the fall. One day, however, because of the finished work of Christ for sinners, "Death shall be no more, neither shall there be mourning, nor crying, nor pain anymore, for the former things have passed away" (Rev. 21:4). No sickness then, therefore.

Theological Soundings

GOD'S WRATH. Those who presume upon God's kindness and delay or refuse to repent of their sin incur God's anger, which Hosea depicts as God's coming like a lion who will "tear and go away" (Hos. 5:14). God holds out mercy to all who repent and return to him, but those who spurn that opportunity will eventually experience an eternal tearing. God's wrath is also depicted as a cup or bowl that the wicked will drink (Ps. 75:8; Rev. 14:10); however, Jesus drank that cup, so that all who come to him may avoid it (Matt. 26:39).

RESTORATION. God delights to bless[2] his children, but he will withhold those blessings, including necessities, to call people out of sin. The root of sin is the pride that seeks to usurp God's authority and live independently from his rule, but when God breaks the illusion of self-sufficiency, sinners are reminded that all their provision comes from him. If repentance comes as a result, the flow of blessing will begin afresh. This pattern was set forth in the Mosaic covenant (Deuteronomy 28) and is observed in the cycle of the judges and in the prophets (e.g., Jer. 3:3; Amos 4:7). It can be glimpsed here in Hosea as well. Following the repentance Hosea prophesies in 6:1–3, the people profess renewed confidence in the Lord, who will "come to us as the showers, as the spring rains that water the earth."

► Personal Implications

Take time to reflect on the implications of Hosea 5:1–6:3 for your own life. Consider what you have learned about the character of God, and make notes below on the (1) *Gospel Glimpses*, (2) *Whole-Bible Connections*, (3) *Theological Soundings*, and (4) this passage as a whole.

1. Gospel Glimpses

2. Whole-Bible Connections

3. Theological Soundings

> ....
> ....
> ....
> ....
> ....
> ....
> ....

4. Hosea 5:1–6:3

> ....
> ....
> ....
> ....
> ....
> ....

▶ **As You Finish This Unit . . .**

Take a moment now to ask for the Lord's help as you continue this study of Hosea. Then look back through the unit and reflect on some key things the Lord may be teaching you.

Definitions

[1] **Resurrection** – The impartation of new, eternal life to a dead person at the end of time (or in the case of Jesus, on the third day after his death). This new life is not a mere resuscitation of the body (as in the case of Lazarus; John 11:1–44) but a transformation of the body to an eternal state (1 Cor. 15:35–58). Both the righteous and the wicked will be resurrected, the former to eternal life and the latter to judgment (John 5:29).

[2] **Bless** – To worship or praise another, especially God; to bestow goodness on another.

WEEK 5: TRANSGRESSORS OF THE COVENANT

Hosea 6:4–7:16

▲

Although God calls his people back to him, Israel scorns him, their life-giver, for idols that take away life. Hosea continues to call the people to repentance, employing various images depicting how ongoing sin has redefined them. Hosea likens Israel to an oven (7:4–7), a partially baked cake (7:8), a senseless dove (7:11–12), and a treacherous bow (7:16).

The Big Picture

Hosea 6:4–7:16 describes the treachery and folly of rejecting God and forsaking his covenant.

> ### Reflection and Discussion

Read through the complete passage for this study, Hosea 6:4–7:16. Then review the questions below and write your notes on them. (For further background, see the *ESV Study Bible*, pages 1631–1633.)

1. The Broken Heart of God (6:4–7:3)

God's grief over the hard-heartedness of his people is clear in the cry to both Ephraim and Judah: "What shall I do with you?" (6:4). The reason for his outburst immediately follows: their love for him is pretense. How is this love described, and how does it contrast with that depicted in 6:1–3?

"My judgment goes forth as the light" (6:5; see also Isa. 51:4). Despite the fickle love of Ephraim and Judah, God continues to call them to repentance. In what way does God's judgment serve as light? See also John 3:19–21.

The sort of love God wants from his people is evidenced in covenant faithfulness and committed pursuit of him (Hos. 6:6). With what has Israel been attempting to placate God; and why, given that sacrifice was required by the covenant, did these efforts displease him? In what ways are we prone to the same thing?

_____

_____

_____

_____

_____

_____

In what way has Israel transgressed the covenant "like Adam" (6:7; compare Gen. 2:16–17; 3:17)? What link is made between Adam and the people of Hosea's day by the apostle Paul in Romans 5:12–18?

_____

_____

_____

_____

_____

_____

"They do not consider that I remember all their evil" (Hos. 7:2). Despite the loud and clear warnings of the prophets, why do the people "not consider" that God sees their sin? Review your notes on Hosea 2:5, 13; 4:6–7, 12; 5:4, 11, 13.

_____

_____

_____

_____

_____

2. Oven, Cake, Dove, and Bow (7:4–16)

Hosea likens Israel to an oven used to bake bread in 7:4, 6, and 7. How does the oven simile[1] show progression over the three times it is used here? What does this convey about the heart of God's people?

_____

_____

_____

_____

_____

Israel is described in 7:8 as being like a "cake not turned," or half-baked. The simile begins when Hosea denounces them for "mixing" with foreigners. What results when God's people become indistinguishable from those who do not know him? Israel had mingled their worship practices with those of the Canaanites. Where do we see something similar in contemporary worship practices?

Knowing or failing to know the Lord is a dominant theme in Hosea (2:8, 20; 5:4; 6:3; 8:2; 9:7; 11:3; 13:4; 14:9). Here, in 7:9, the people do not know they are being destroyed by the very thing from which they seek strength. What light does this shed on the nature of sin?

Hosea also likens Israel to a dove, "silly and without sense" (7:11). What is Hosea conveying with this imagery? Why has Israel been "calling to Egypt" and "going to Assyria"?

Rather than turning to the Lord wholeheartedly, the people give themselves more fully to Baal, "gash[ing] themselves" in hopes of economic gain (7:14; see also 1 Kings 18:26–29). What lies behind the people's bent toward self-destruction, and how is this folly exposed in Hosea 7:16?

Read through the following three sections on *Gospel Glimpses*, *Whole-Bible Connections*, and *Theological Soundings*. Then take time to consider the *Personal Implications* these sections may have for you.

Gospel Glimpses

LIGHT. "My judgment goes forth as the light" (Hos. 6:5). God's light exposes the true nature of sin—in Israel's case, idolatry. This is a great mercy, for apart from exposure to God's light, we cannot recognize the nature of sin. The light of God's judgment has been manifested most fully in the person of Christ, the "light of the world," and whoever welcomes exposure to this light "will not walk in darkness, but will have the light of life" (John 8:12). Those who reject Jesus remain in spiritual darkness (John 3:19). Yet Jesus holds out his light to all who will come (John 12:46).

HEALING. Israel has chosen the sickness and wounding of sin (Hos. 5:13), yet despite their rebellion, God holds out the hope of healing (7:1), pointing forward to the work of Christ. During his earthly ministry Jesus healed the sick and the wounded to point people to his ultimate purpose—the healing of sin for all who come to him in faith. He bore our wounds on the cross in order to heal us.

Whole-Bible Connections

HARVEST. "For you also, O Judah, a harvest is appointed, when I restore the fortunes of my people" (Hos. 6:11). Harvest time was intended to be a celebratory time of feasting and thanksgiving to the Lord for his bountiful provision, and the perpetual cycle of spiritual reaping and sowing continues in every age (Gal. 6:7). Jesus' parable of the sower defines God's kingdom in agricultural terms and teaches that only seed sown in good soil will survive to the harvest (Matt. 13:1–8, 18–23). Other parables use similar imagery (Mark 4:26–29, 30–32), and the final judgment is depicted as a great harvest (Rev. 14:14–20).

WHOLEHEARTEDNESS. "They do not cry to me from the heart" (Hos. 7:14). God desires true, heartfelt worship from his people. God's requirement of wholeheartedness springs from his relational nature, which comes through clearly in Hosea's marriage imagery. True love seeks and pursues the object of its affection with passion, as God does through his prophet, and he is grieved when the one he loves fails to reciprocate. Wholeheartedness toward God is developed by immersion in Scripture (Ps. 119:2, 10, 34, 69, 145) and obedience (Jer. 24:7). The apostle Paul gave new-covenant expression to such devotion: "For me to live is Christ," and, "I count everything as loss because of the surpassing worth of knowing Christ Jesus my Lord" (Phil. 1:21; 3:8).

EGYPT. "This shall be their derision in the land of Egypt" (Hos. 7:16). This reference to Egypt is metaphorical for Israel's bondage there prior to the exodus, and is used here by Hosea to again display how far Israel has fallen. Through the exodus God ransomed his people out of Egyptian slavery, which prefigured ransom and exodus from slavery to sin. Bondage in Egypt as a metaphor for bondage to sin is evident in the prophet's warnings against returning there (7:11; 12:1). Hosea also uses returning to Egypt as a metaphor for judgment (7:16; 8:13; 9:3, 6; 12:1). Yet God triumphed over the powers of Egypt and brought his people out, just as he has done for sinners through Christ. Jesus' personal history repeated aspects of Israel's national history, including going down to and coming up from Egypt, and Matthew cites Hosea in this regard (Matt. 2:13–15).

Theological Soundings

REMEMBRANCE. "I remember all their evil" (Hos. 7:2). Unlike Israel, a family that has failed to know God (2:8; 5:4; 11:3) and even themselves (7:9), the Lord knows everything about his people, which is why Hosea can address them at the level of their hearts and motives (e.g., 4:6–7; 5:4, 11; 7:14). God's knowing, his remembrance of their evil, serves also as an indictment, a way of declaring his people's guilt (7:2; 8:13; 9:9). Nevertheless, God is willing to put aside his memory of their sin and forget, if his people will only turn back to him, as David did when he prayed, "Have mercy on me, O God; . . . blot out my transgressions" (Ps. 51:1). Through the death and resurrection of Christ, the sins of God's people have been forgotten for all time (Heb. 8:12; 10:17).

COVENANT. "They transgressed the covenant" (Hos. 6:7). The sins and curses pronounced in the Sinai covenant match the warnings of the prophet: the end of agricultural prosperity, military disaster, foreign exile, and return to slavery in Egypt. The overarching problem in Israel throughout their history was failure to keep the covenant (Deut. 29:25). For that reason, God in his mercy provided a new covenant, one in which he fulfilled the terms on both sides—his and theirs. Jesus is the mediator of the new covenant, "that those who are called may receive the promised eternal inheritance, since a death has occurred that redeems them from the transgressions committed under the first covenant" (Heb. 9:15).

Personal Implications

Take time to reflect on the implications of Hosea 6:4–7:16 for your own life today. Consider what you have learned that might lead you to a greater love for God. Make notes below on the personal implications for your walk with the Lord of the (1) *Gospel Glimpses*, (2) *Whole-Bible Connections*, (3) *Theological Soundings*, and (4) this passage as a whole.

1. Gospel Glimpses

2. Whole-Bible Connections

3. Theological Soundings

4. Hosea 6:4–7:16

_____

_____

_____

_____

_____

_____

_____

> ## As You Finish This Unit . . .

Take a moment now to ask for the Lord's help as you continue in this study of Hosea. Then look back through this unit to reflect on some key things the Lord is teaching you.

Definition

[1] **Simile** – A figure of speech, often seen in poetry, that compares two objects, often using "like" or "as," even though they are not actually the same thing. A biblical example is in Psalm 1:3: "He is like a tree planted by streams of water."

WEEK 6: ISRAEL'S HYPOCRISY

Hosea 8:1–14

▲

> ## The Place of the Passage

Israel claims to know God, but their practices belie their claim, and in this chapter the Lord exposes their hypocrisy, citing specific violations of God's law. God's people have been unfaithful to him, setting up leaders without consulting God, participating in idol worship, and forming alliances with foreign powers. Far from knowing the Lord, "Israel has forgotten his Maker" (8:14).

> ## The Big Picture

In Hosea 8:1–14, God exposes the hypocrisy of his people, who claim to know him yet continue in blatant, unrepentant sin.

> ### Reflection and Discussion

Read through Hosea 8:1–14, the focus of this week's study. Following this, review the questions below and write your responses concerning this section of the book of Hosea. (For further background, see the *ESV Study Bible*, pages 1633–1634.)

1. Israel's False Cry (8:1–3)

"One like a vulture is over the house of the LORD, because they have transgressed . . . and rebelled" (8:1). A foreign power has ascended over Israel, likely Assyria. Based on all Hosea has said thus far in his prophecy, how has Israel's sin brought about foreign dominance?

God's people claim that all is well in their relationship with the Lord: "My God, we—Israel—know you" (8:2). What led them to believe all was well, despite the clear words of the prophet to the contrary? Read Matthew 7:21–23 and Luke 6:46–49, where Jesus warns that not everyone who claims to know him truly does. What measure does Jesus use in those passages to determine one's knowledge of God? Read James 1:22–25. What language in that passage is similar to what you have observed in Hosea?

Because "Israel has spurned the good" (Hos. 8:3), God will "spurn" their idol (v. 5), disillusioning his people as to its power. What does it mean to "spurn" something or someone? How is the term used covenantally in Leviticus 26:12–17, 40–45?

----

2. Incapable of Innocence (8:4–6)

"They made kings, but not through me. They set up princes, but I knew it not" (8:4). Concerning leadership, how have God's people offended him? Throughout Scripture God's omniscience[1] is clearly portrayed, so what is meant here that God "knew it not"?

"How long will they be incapable of innocence?" (8:5). The Lord's question, posed through Hosea, is rhetorical. It is an expression of the utter depravity[2] of man. How do both Genesis 2:17; 3:1–7 and Romans 7:7–25 provide the answer?

"A craftsman made it; it is not God" (8:6). The calf of Samaria (vv. 5, 6) is the idol Baal, who was often depicted as standing on a bull. Read the story of the golden calf in Exodus 32:1–4. What echoes of that story do you see here in Hosea 8:4–6?

2. Reaping the Whirlwind (8:7–14)

Hosea again makes use of agricultural imagery: "They sow the wind, and they shall reap the whirlwind" (8:7). Why is "wind" an apt way to describe the sin Israel is sowing? (See also 4:19.) The imagery continues, depicting a worthless harvest; even "if it were to yield, strangers would devour it." How do these images reinforce what Hosea has said about the nature of idolatry?

"Were I to write for him my laws by the ten thousands, they would be regarded as a strange thing" (8:12). Israel cannot blame God for their failure to know him. God has made his ways plain. Read Deuteronomy 4:5–8. How does that passage point directly to the source of Israel's failure? Where do we see similar arguments in our culture, our churches, and ourselves today?

"I will send a fire . . . and it shall devour her strongholds" (8:14). By trusting in idols, God's people have forgotten him and have come to rely on false foundations for security. But God will destroy these "strongholds," demonstrating that he is the only reliable security for his people. How does something or someone besides God become a stronghold in one's heart and life? How did it happen to God's people in Hosea's day?

Read through the following three sections on *Gospel Glimpses, Whole-Bible Connections*, and *Theological Soundings*. Then take time to consider the *Personal Implications* these sections may have for you.

Gospel Glimpses

KING. "They made kings, but not through me" (Hos. 8:4). God has always been king over his people, but they rejected him as their king (1 Sam. 8:7). Even so, God had planned for an earthly kingship (Deut. 17:14–20), eventually establishing the kingly line through David and his descendants. David brought blessing to the nation, but his sin and those of the kings following him pointed to the need for Christ, the King of kings. Only King Jesus can offer the protection, deliverance, and provision his people need, and he procured all that on the cross, so that one day he will gather all his people together, and they will declare, "Great and amazing are your deeds, O Lord God the Almighty! Just and true are your ways, O King of the nations!" (Rev. 15:3).

REDEMPTION. Hosea 8 trumpets the reality of God's judgment, which will soon come and carry Israel back to Egypt (v. 13). The return to Egypt, the place of earlier bondage, points to the covenant failure of God's people. A greater redemption was needed. Jesus Christ, who was called out of Egypt (Hos. 11:1; Matt. 2:15), provided that redemption through his sinless life, death on the cross, and resurrection. With Christ came a new covenant (Heb. 8:8–9). In Christ God's people are redeemed, their bondage to sin forever broken.

Whole-Bible Connections

VESSEL. Israel had become a "useless vessel" (Hos. 8:8) by adopting the practices of pagans. Throughout the Bible, vessels are used metaphorically to describe human usefulness or lack thereof. A useful vessel is one that has been refined and purified (Prov. 25:4; 2 Tim. 2:21). Clay was a common medium for vessels, rendering them breakable but also increasing their usefulness as a means to showcase God's glory: "We have this treasure in jars of clay, to show that the surpassing power belongs to God and not to us" (2 Cor. 4:7). Ultimately, it is God who does the shaping of individual vessels for his own purposes (Jer. 18:1–4; Rom. 9:21).

STRONGHOLD. The most secure place in ancient cities was the citadel, called the "stronghold," which is how God wants his people to view him (Ps. 27:1), but sin had twisted Israel's view of where strength could be found (Hos. 8:14). God is a stronghold on behalf of the weak and oppressed in times of trouble (Pss. 9:9; 18:2; 37:9; 144:2; Isa. 25:4), so looking for strength elsewhere is folly (Gen. 11:1–9; Isa. 2:12–15; 1 John 3:8). In Christ, God exposed and defeated the strongholds of evil and death (1 Cor. 15:54–57). Israel stopped looking to God as their stronghold and were tricked into reliance on false securities. The history of God's people proves the reality that we come to trust what we worship. But there is only one true security: "O LORD, my strength and my stronghold, my refuge in the day of trouble, to you shall the nations come" (Jer. 16:19).

Theological Soundings

GOD'S LAW. God gave the law as fatherly instruction to shape his people into a community of faith, holiness, and love. Sadly, Israel's history is a record of continual law-breaking. But God had promised a new covenant to write the law on people's hearts (Jer. 31:31–33). Through Christ, the mediator of the new covenant, God's people become a "letter from Christ . . . written not with ink but with the Spirit of the living God, not on tablets of stone but on tablets of human hearts" (2 Cor. 3:3).

DEPRAVITY. "How long will they be incapable of innocence?" (Hos. 8:5). This rhetorical question points to the utter depravity of man, but it contains a gospel glimpse as well. Mankind has been incapable of innocence since the fall, when Adam and Eve ate from the tree of the knowledge of good and evil. The innocence lost at the fall and addressed here in Hosea pertains not to intellectual knowledge but to purity and holiness. Left to himself, man is incapable of moral purity; however, lost purity was regained through the perfectly innocent man, Christ Jesus, and is restored in those united to him by faith: "It was indeed fitting that we should have such a high priest, holy, innocent, unstained, separated from sinners, and exalted above the heavens" (Heb. 7:26).

Personal Implications

Take time to reflect on the implications of Hosea 8:1–14 for your own life today. Consider what you have learned that will strengthen your walk with Christ. Make notes below on the personal implications for your walk with the Lord of the (1) *Gospel Glimpses*, (2) *Whole-Bible Connections*, (3) *Theological Soundings*, and (4) this passage as a whole.

1. Gospel Glimpses

2. Whole-Bible Connections

3. Theological Soundings

4. Hosea 8:1–14

> ## As You Finish This Unit . . .

Take a moment now to ask for the Lord's blessing as you continue in this study of Hosea. Reflect on some key things the Lord is teaching you.

Definitions

[1] **Omniscience** – An attribute of God that describes his complete knowledge and understanding of all things at all times.

[2] **Depravity** – The sinful condition of human nature apart from grace, whereby humans are inclined to serve their own will and desires and to reject God's rule.

WEEK 7: NO WORSHIP IN A FOREIGN LAND

Hosea 9:1–9

The Place of the Passage

Hosea 9:1–9 is a reiteration of the prophet's primary message: because God's people have refused to repent of their spiritual adultery, God will punish them. The idols to which Israel has turned will fail, and the foreign powers she has sought security from will bring her ruin. However, God's punishment is not meant ultimately to destroy but to redeem. In God's sending the people away from the land, to a place where they will not be able to make sacrifices to the Lord, he will give his people over to what they think they want in order to show them what they really need.

The Big Picture

Hosea 9:1–9 shows that God is just in punishing unrepentant sinners yet holds out mercy as he executes his justice.

> ## Reflection and Discussion

Read through the complete passage for this study, Hosea 9:1–9. Then review the questions below and write your notes on them. (For further background, see the *ESV Study Bible*, pages 1634–1635.)

1. No Rejoicing (9:1–6)

"Rejoice not, O Israel!" declares Hosea (9:1). God's people have been living as if nothing were amiss, carrying out the rituals of worshiping the Lord while simultaneously serving idols and attempting to blend with pagans.[1] But the Lord knows their hearts and that their worship is pretense. In what way is the call to stop rejoicing a merciful call?

In what way has Israel "loved a prostitute's wages" (9:1)? How do Deuteronomy 23:18 and Jeremiah 44:21–23 shed light on the significance of Hosea's indictment?

"They shall not remain in the land of the LORD" (Hos. 9:3). Inheriting the land of Canaan was part and parcel of God's covenant promises to his people. Read Deuteronomy 8:1–20, where Moses sets out covenant stipulations for enjoying the Promised Land, along with God's intentions for his people there. Why was the pending loss of this land such a dire prospect?

_____

_____

_____

_____

_____

_____

When God's people are taken out of the Promised Land, they "shall return to Egypt" and "eat unclean food in Assyria" (Hos. 9:3). Hosea uses covenant language to indicate that Israel's faulty political strategy involving Egypt and Assyria will backfire. God brought the people out of Egypt, and he can just as easily send them back by lifting his covenant protection. The covenant also designated certain foods as clean and unclean.[2] What is indicated by Hosea's prophecy that the people will be forced to eat unclean food? (For background, see Leviticus 11, esp. vv. 44–45.)

_____

_____

_____

_____

_____

"They are going away from destruction" (Hos. 9:6). With a note of irony, Hosea indicates that the people believe they are pursuing a safe course. The opposite is true, however, because they are actually running toward destruction. What other coming disasters are described in verse 6? How does each one directly connect to Israel's current sinful pursuits?

_____

_____

_____

_____

_____

2. As in the Days of Gibeah (9:7–9)

"The prophet is a fool" (9:7). Hosea's reference pertains either to the futility of the prophets' mission or to how the people perceive the dire warnings. Either way, the image springs from the people's "great iniquity and great hatred." By now we are well aware of Israel's iniquity, yet for the first time Hosea speaks of the people's hatred—twice in this section (vv. 7–8). As you consider Exodus 20:4–5; Proverbs 8:13; and Matthew 6:24, how do you think we should understand this reference to hatred? As you consider the specific charges against Israel thus far in the book, where and how does hatred factor in?

"The prophet is the watchman of Ephraim" (Hos. 9:8). The prophets were God's watchmen to warn God's people of impending catastrophe (see Isa. 21:6–9; Ezek. 3:16–17, 33:1–9; Hab. 2:1). Why, according to Hosea here, could faithfulness in carrying out this call be done only in the strength of the Lord?

While all corruption is vile, Hosea speaks to the depth of Israel's sin when he says that God's people have "deeply corrupted themselves as in the days of Gibeah" (Hos. 9:9). For the backstory of Hosea's reference, read Judges 19. What do you see in the Judges story that points to why Hosea references it in his prophecy? As you examine that dark incident from Israel's history, what correlations do you find there to the condition of Israel in Hosea's day?

"He will remember their iniquity; he will punish their sins" (Hos. 9:9). God's judgment draws near, as Hosea has warned repeatedly. As you reflect on his indictment in this section, what reason do you see for why this repeated warning goes unheeded? What truths are reinforced here about the effects of sin on the heart?

Read through the following three sections on *Gospel Glimpses, Whole-Bible Connections,* and *Theological Soundings.* Then take time to consider the *Personal Implications* these sections may have for you.

► Gospel Glimpses

JESUS AS PROPHET. The prophets were scorned by a sinful people and their message was largely disregarded (Hos. 9:7). The impotence of the Old Testament prophets to effect change at a heart level shows the need for a prophet whose message, although rejected by many, could not ultimately be ignored. That such a prophet would one day come was foretold to Moses (Deut. 18:15–19) and fulfilled in Jesus, God's great prophet (Acts 3:22–24).

PLEASING SACRIFICE. Sacrifices were required under the terms of the old covenant, but God was displeased with sacrifices offered in pretense from defiled hearts (Hos. 9:4). Even when offered rightly, sin necessitated that the sacrifices be offered continually. Every human heart is defiled, which is why all those sacrifices failed to satisfy the requirements of a holy God (Heb. 10:4, 11); they served only to expose the need for a better sacrifice. Only one sacrifice has ever satisfied God—that of his Son, Jesus (Heb. 9:26; 10:5–10).

► Whole-Bible Connections

THORNS. Using an agricultural metaphor, Hosea warns the unrepentant that "thorns shall be in their tents" (Hos. 9:6). From the time of the fall, thorns are a sign of God's curse (Gen. 3:18; Isa. 34:13; Jer. 12:13; Heb. 6:8) and of uselessness. In the parable of the sower Jesus describes the fruitlessness of those who allow the thorns of worldliness to choke the Word (Matt. 13:22). The curse indicated by thorns came down on the head of Jesus (John 19:2, 5), who was forced to wear a crown of thorns at his crucifixion—and by submitting to the thorn curse, he removed it from God's people for all time.

EXILE. After the fall into sin, Adam and Eve were exiled from God's presence (Gen. 3:23). Afterward, sin and exile were forever linked. God promised his people abundant life in the Promised Land, but along with it came the stipulation of obedience. Rebellion would lead to exile from the land and from God's presence (Lev. 26:33; Deut. 28:36–41), a punishment about which Hosea issues urgent warnings. His warnings went unheeded, however, and God's people were exiled to Babylon. All humanity is spiritually exiled from God due to sin, but Jesus, in his death, accepted exile from God's presence to enable us to return (Mark 15:34). Through his death and resurrection we can enjoy God's presence now, with no fear of banishment. The way back to Eden has been opened, and one day those united to Christ by faith will be with him face-to-face in an Eden made new (Rev. 21:1–22:5).

Theological Soundings

GOD'S IMMANENCE. Under the old covenant, Israel enjoyed God's presence by observing the covenantal terms of worship, which included sacrificial offerings and participation in appointed feasts. So, when Hosea tells Israel that "they shall eat unclean food in Assyria" (Hos. 9:3) and no longer "pour drink offerings of wine to the LORD" (9:4), he is warning them about being cut off from the protective fellowship of God. Hosea wants Israel to consider the ramifications: "What will you do on the day of the appointed festival, and on the day of the feast of the LORD?" (9:5). The horror of exile has less to do with land than with being cut off from God's presence. God delights in drawing near to his people; this quality, called his *immanence*, is part of his very nature. Sin separates us all from the enjoyment of our relational God, yet through Christ he has forever closed that wide chasm (Eph. 2:13).

MAN'S CORRUPTION. Israel's depravity has been clear throughout Hosea's prophecy, yet here in Hosea 9 its depths are plumbed even further. The people are characterized by "great iniquity and great hatred" (v. 7) and "have deeply corrupted themselves as in the days of Gibeah" (v. 9). The episode at Gibeah involved rampant lust, sexual perversion, murder, and callous disregard of both the Lord and human beings (see Judges 19), as also reflected in the condition of Sodom before the Lord destroyed it. This is the point to which God's people had now come. Apart from divine restraint, there are no limits on where sin will take us. That is why the psalmist cries, "Keep back your servant from presumptuous sins; let them not have dominion over me!" (Ps. 19:13). Concerning sin the apostle Paul writes, "I do not do what I want, but I do the very thing I hate," and in his sin-wretchedness he cries, "Who will deliver me from this body of death?" (Rom. 7:15, 24). We are utterly helpless against the power of sin apart from the intervening hand of God; but he *has* intervened, which is why Paul can joyfully answer his own question: "Thanks be to God through Jesus Christ our Lord!" (Rom. 7:25).

Personal Implications

Take time to reflect on the implications of Hosea 9:1–9 for your own life today. Consider what you have learned that might lead you to see your sin, repent of it, and cast yourself more fully on Christ as Savior. Make notes below on the personal implications for your walk with the Lord of the (1) *Gospel Glimpses*, (2) *Whole-Bible Connections*, (3) *Theological Soundings*, and (4) this passage as a whole.

1. Gospel Glimpses

2. Whole-Bible Connections

3. Theological Soundings

4. Hosea 9:1–9

As You Finish This Unit . . .

Take a moment now to ask for the Lord's help as you continue in this study. Take a moment also to look back through this unit and reflect on some key things that the Lord is teaching you.

Definitions

[1] **Paganism** – Any belief system that does not acknowledge the God of the Bible as the one true God. Atheism, polytheism, pantheism, animism, and humanism, as well as numerous other religious systems, can all be classified as forms of paganism.

[2] **Clean/unclean** – The ceremonial, spiritual, or moral state of a person or object, affected by a variety of factors. The terms are primarily related to the concept of holiness and have little to do with actual physical cleanliness. The Mosaic law declared certain foods and animals unclean, and a person became unclean if he or she came in contact with certain substances or objects, such as a dead body. Jesus declared all foods clean (Mark 7:19), and Peter's vision in Acts 10 shows that no person is ceremonially unclean simply because he or she is a Gentile.

Week 8: Unfaithful Israel

Hosea 9:10–11:11

▲

The Place of the Passage

In Hosea 9:10–11:11 Hosea uses four images to remind Israel of their relationship with the Lord in earlier times. God's people were once like grapes growing in the wilderness (9:10–17), fruitful and flourishing. They were also like a luxuriant vine (10:1–10), an image meant to remind Israel that they had once prospered under the Lord. At one time, Israel was like a trained calf (10:11–15); they willingly obeyed God. Finally, through the image of a toddler (11:1–11), Hosea reminds them of God's fatherly care. But because Israel has rejected all of that, unavoidable consequences are coming.

The Big Picture

In Hosea 9:10–11:11 God reminds his people of the covenant blessings they have abandoned in favor of idols.

> ### Reflection and Discussion

Read the entire text for this week's study, Hosea 9:10–11:11. Then review the following questions and write your notes on them. (For further background, see the *ESV Study Bible*, pages 1635–1639.)

1. Grapes in the Wilderness (9:10–17)

"Like grapes in the wilderness, I found Israel" (9:10). This section reflects on an earlier time in Israel's covenantal relationship with the Lord. What contrast is presented in this image, and what do you think it is meant to convey?

"But they came to Baal-peor" (9:10). Despite the incomparable blessings of living in covenant with the Lord, Israel repeatedly turned away from God to idols, especially to the fertility god Baal. Here Hosea refers to a specific occasion of spiritual adultery that occurred at Peor. Read the details of that episode in Numbers 25:1–5. What tempted the people away from the Lord in that incident, and what does Hosea 9:10 add to our understanding of it?

Idolatry affects not only the idol worshipers but also subsequent generations, which is made clear in this section. Forsaking God to worship Baal will result in the eventual demise of the people (9:11–14, 16). How does this inevitable outcome expose the irony of Baal worship?

----

2. A Luxuriant Vine (10:1–10)

"Israel is a luxuriant vine that yields its fruit" (10:1). Hosea uses another image, that of a fruitful vine, to remind Israel of better days (see also Ps. 80:8–11). Historically, their abandonment of the Lord coincided with prosperity, a connection also made in Jeremiah: "I spoke to you in your prosperity, but you said, 'I will not listen'" (Jer. 22:21). In what way could prosperous conditions test one's faithfulness to the Lord?

Hosea foretells the end of the northern kingdom, when the people will have no king. The people will be given what they want: "We have no king, for we do not fear the LORD; and a king—what could he do for us?" (Hos. 10:3). Their words harken back to the days when Israel rejected God's kingship in favor of being ruled by a human king (1 Sam. 8:4–7). And while God did establish a monarchy for them—the line of David—it proved to be woefully inadequate. By means of this long, unsuccessful history, God will eventually restore the hearts of his people to acknowledge his rightful kingship over them. Israel's growing despair with human kingship is evident here in Hosea 10. What do we see in verses 4–9 that evidences this despair?

God is going to discipline his wayward people, using the nations to do so (10:10). What does that reveal about how God works in the world?

3. A Trained Calf (10:11–15)

Israel is fixated on a fertility idol, so Hosea addresses them with agrarian images. The image of a trained calf (10:11) is another allusion to Israel's beginnings. The Lord spared his people the yoke; they loved to thresh in his field (see Deut. 25:4). But that freedom was abused, so the people will have to be harnessed. What will result if God's people submit to the yoke of his discipline?

The law of sowing and reaping is clear in Hosea 10:13. Because Israel has sown iniquity, she will reap injustice; by trusting in man rather than God, Israel has come to believe lies rather than truth. Think of a time when you "trusted in your own way" rather than in the Lord. What did you reap as a result? How would you define the "fruit of lies"?

4. A Toddler (11:1–11)

"When Israel was a child, I loved him" (11:1). The Lord is not only their king and husband; he is also their father and *has* been since forming them as his own special people (see Ex. 4:22–23). He aches over them with a father's concern for a wayward, rebellious child. Read Luke 15:11–32, Jesus' parable of the prodigal son. How does that parable reveal God's intentions toward Israel in the discipline they are about to undergo? See also Hebrews 12:5–11.

By means of the toddler image (11:1–4), Hosea recounts how God cared for Israel when the people were small and weak. What word pictures does the prophet use to describe God's care in this passage, and what do these pictures convey?

Read through the following three sections on *Gospel Glimpses, Whole-Bible Connections,* and *Theological Soundings*. Then take time to consider the *Personal Implications* these sections may have for you.

▶ Gospel Glimpses

VINE. "Israel is a luxuriant vine that yields its fruit" (Hos. 10:1). God intended his people to flourish under his care and produce fruit, making every provision for his choice vine to thrive (e.g., Isa. 5:1–7; 27:2–6). But instead of maturing into a ripened vineyard, Israel's growth was choked by sin (Ezek. 15:1–8). Israel's failure to flourish points us to Jesus, the "true vine" (John 15:1–5). Those who abide in him never fail to produce fruit.

YOKE. God delivered his people from the yoke of slavery in Egypt and set them free to live with him in covenant obedience. But that freedom was abused; Israel "plowed iniquity" (Hos. 10:13). Therefore, a painful harness was needed (see Ps. 32:9). All along, however, God's intention was for Israel to sow the seeds of righteousness and reap a crop of steadfast love (Hos. 10:12). In contrast to the painful but necessary yokes of Israel's history is the gentle yoke of Jesus Christ, which his people are invited to wear (Matt. 11:28). The yoke of Jesus not only instructs but also unburdens and leads to rest (vv. 29–30).

SON OF GOD. The people of Israel rejected their divine Father, but God's greater Son, Jesus, did not. The New Testament cites Hosea 11:1 to show that Jesus is the true and faithful Son of God (Matt. 2:15). Jesus' perfect sonship is imputed[1] to all who come to God through him, "for those whom he foreknew he also predestined to be conformed to the image of his Son, in order that he might be the firstborn among many brothers" (Rom. 8:29).

Whole-Bible Connections

PROSPERITY IS DANGEROUS. "The more his fruit increased, the more altars he built" (Hos. 10:1). Material prosperity is spiritually risky. Even before entering the Promised Land, Moses had warned Israel to beware this danger (Deut. 8:11–14). But the warnings were disregarded; as God's people prospered, they forgot God. This risk applies to God's people in every age. Material abundance can breed the illusion of self-sufficiency, thereby blinding one to the reality that all things come from God's hand. Jesus warned about this danger (Matt. 19:23–24; Luke 12:13–21), as did the apostles (1 Tim. 6:9–10). Wisdom and humility are essential qualities for wealthy believers, an attitude reflected in the prayer of Agur in Proverbs (Prov. 30:8–9).

SOWING/REAPING. The principle of sowing and reaping has been woven by God into the fabric of creation. One reaps what one sows, whether in farming or in spiritual matters. In the Old Testament, agricultural fruitfulness reflected spiritual fruitfulness, and crop failure mirrored spiritual failure (Deut. 28:1–4, 15–18). Hosea uses the imagery of failed crops to expose Israel's sin and its consequences (Hos. 10:4), and because Israel has "plowed iniquity," she has "reaped injustice" and "eaten the fruit of lies" (v. 13). If Israel would sow righteousness instead, she would "reap steadfast love" (v. 12). The principle of sowing and reaping is also featured in Jesus' parables, e.g., the sower (Matt. 13:1–9); the weeds (Matt. 13:24–30); and the mustard seed (Matt. 13:31–32); and the apostle Paul stated it clearly (Gal. 6:7).

Theological Soundings

SOVEREIGNTY.[2] "When I please, I will discipline them, and nations shall be gathered against them" (Hos. 10:10). God governs whatever comes to pass in the world and in the lives of his people, yet his plans are typically carried out through secondary causes, sometimes through hostile powers. By this means, God's authority is revealed to both his friends and his foes, which was clearly the case with Pharaoh during Israel's enslavement in Egypt (Rom. 9:17). Ultimately, God's use of hostile men to bring about his will is shown in the death of Jesus: he was "delivered up according to the definite plan and foreknowledge of God," but God did this through the actions of "lawless men" (Acts 2:23; see also Luke 22:22; Acts 3:13–16; 4:27–28).

DIVINE LOVE. God's choice of Israel was based solely on his love for them (Deut. 7:8; 10:15). Israel spurned that love repeatedly, but their sin did not crush it. Whereas human love is circumstantial and often fickle, divine love is constant and freely given, leaving God vulnerable to pain, which he clearly exhibits in Israel's spurning of his affection: "How can I give you up, O Ephraim? . . .

My heart recoils within me" (Hos. 11:8). These emotional outpourings show that the Lord's affection outweighs Israel's ingratitude. God's love is shown most supremely in the sending of his Son, whom he sacrificed in order to save sinners (John 3:16). Through Jesus, God calls to himself those who have not sought him (Rom. 8:28–30).

Personal Implications

Take time to reflect on the implications of Hosea 9:10–11:11 for your own life today. Consider what you have learned that might lead you to respond more fully to God's love for you in Christ. Make notes below on the personal implications for your walk with the Lord of the (1) *Gospel Glimpses*, (2) *Whole-Bible Connections*, (3) *Theological Soundings*, and (4) this passage as a whole.

1. Gospel Glimpses

2. Whole-Bible Connections

3. Theological Soundings

4. Hosea 9:10–11:11

As You Finish This Unit . . .

Take a moment now to ask for the Lord's blessing as you continue in this study, and then reflect on what the Lord is teaching you.

Definitions

[1] **Impute** – To attribute something to someone or credit it to his or her account. Often refers to God's crediting to every believer the righteousness of Jesus Christ.

[2] **Sovereignty** – Supreme and independent power and authority. Sovereignty over all things is a distinctive attribute of God (1 Tim. 6:15–16). He directs all things to carry out his purposes (Rom. 8:28–29).

WEEK 9: MISPLACED DEPENDENCE

Hosea 11:12–12:14

▲

Although Judah, the southern kingdom, has made some effort to remain faithful to God, Judah eventually follows the path of the northern kingdom into apostasy and is also destroyed (see 11:12–12:2). How could God's people have fallen so far when they had the Lord as their God? The remainder of the passage (12:3–14) recounts the Lord's enduring kindness toward his people despite their ingratitude, which serves to show them that they are solely to blame for their plight.

The Big Picture

Hosea 11:12–12:14 shows us that God's kind character and determination to bless are not thwarted by the sin and unworthiness of his people.

> ## Reflection and Discussion

Read through the complete text for this study, Hosea 11:12–12:14. Then review the questions below and write your notes on them. (For further background, see the *ESV Study Bible*, pages 1639–1640.)

1. Dependence on Alliances (11:12–12:1)

"Ephraim has surrounded me with lies . . . but Judah still walks with God" (11:12). Judah is compared favorably here with Israel, or Ephraim, despite indictments leveled against Judah earlier in the book (5:5, 10, 12, 14; 6:4; 8:14). The favorable comparison is likely due to the fact that Judah, unlike Israel, had some good kings. Read 2 Kings 18:1–12, which recounts King Hezekiah's reign over Judah, a reign that began during the time of Hosea. In direct contrast to the failures of Ephraim's kings as set forth in Hosea, what good did King Hezekiah carry out?

"Israel feeds on the wind," Hosea declares (12:1), and moreover, she "pursues" it. What does this image convey? See also Psalm 78:39; Ecclesiastes 1:14; 2:11; and Isaiah 26:18.

A repeated indictment in this section is that Israel has "surrounded" the Lord with lies (11:12) and multiplied falsehood (12:1). In what way are they lying to the Lord?

---

2. The Past, the Present, and the Future (12:2–14)

"The LORD has an indictment against Judah" (12:2). Although Judah has not rejected the covenant as fully as Israel (11:12), Judah is far from being right with the Lord. At the time of Hosea, the two nations had been separate for nearly two hundred years, but they were following the same downward course. Hosea begins this section by addressing Judah, recounting episodes from the life of Jacob, the forefather of both kingdoms. Jacob's birth is mentioned (see Gen. 25:21–26), as well as events during his adult life (Gen. 32:24–31; 35:9–15). What do these accounts in Genesis convey about both Jacob and God?

"The LORD is his memorial name" (Hos. 12:5). The reference to a memorial name is meant to remind God's people of the relationship he established with their forefathers, the patriarchs (see Ex. 3:15). What aspects of that covenantal relationship are seen in Hosea 12:6?

Sin twists one's understanding and affections. How is this evidenced in Hosea 12:7–8?

The Lord reminds Israel and Judah that, through the prophets, he has always provided ample guidance (12:10). Therefore, God's people cannot claim insufficient knowledge or revelation as an excuse for their misplaced trust in idols or foreign powers. According to Deuteronomy 4:5–6, 32–36 and Psalm 147:19–20, what were God's prophets intended to provide for his people? How was this both a privilege and a responsibility?

The patriarch Jacob, also called "Israel," is referenced again in Hosea 12:12–13. Hosea recalls events that led Jacob to father the 12 tribes of Israel (see Gen. 28:1–5; 29:1–30), from whom Hosea's audience descended. As you reflect on this time in the life of Jacob, where do you see signs of God's grace?

Hosea 12:13 reveals a vital aspect of the prophetic office—that of guarding God's people. The reference here is to Moses, who led Israel out of Egypt and through the 40-year period in the wilderness. How was the prophet intended to serve as a guard for God's people? (See Deut. 18:15, 18–19.)

Read through the following three sections on *Gospel Glimpses, Whole-Bible Connections,* and *Theological Soundings.* Then take time to consider the *Personal Implications* these sections may have for you.

Gospel Glimpses

GUARDED. Jacob guarded sheep in order to win his bride (Hos. 12:12), and the Lord sent prophets to guard his people (12:13). The security Israel craved would have been theirs if only they had remained under their divinely appointed guardian. The law, too, served as a guardian for the people until the coming of Christ, when the new covenant was instituted (Gal. 3:24–25). Under the new covenant, God's people are guarded by faith (Rom. 3:21–22), kept safe until Christ returns (1 Pet. 1:5). Those who believe will not fall away because the Lord himself is their guard (2 Thess. 3:3; Jude 24).

PARDON. "The LORD . . . will punish Jacob according to his ways" (Hos. 12:2). God is patient and merciful, and he is also just. The punishments about to befall Ephraim and later Judah flow from God's justice and prefigure the end of all who refuse to serve him (Rev. 20:11–15). The judgment that befell God's people points to their need for a Savior, one who can satisfy the justice whereby every human is condemned. In Jesus, God's justice has been satisfied forever for all who put their faith in him (1 John 2:1–2); the perfect righteousness of Christ is imputed to believers. God is just, yet he is also the justifier of all who put faith in Christ (Rom. 3:26).

Whole-Bible Connections

WAITING ON GOD. Living in covenant relationship with the Lord entails a commitment to love and justice as well as the humility to "wait continually for your God" (Hos. 12:6), which is precisely what God's people were refusing to do (compare Isa. 8:17). Waiting on God involves trusting that he is in control of all things. No other power or circumstance is determinative. Waiting also includes obedience, even when adhering to God's ways seems counterintuitive. Those who wait for the Lord will never be ashamed (Ps. 25:3), and their trust will be rewarded (Ps. 37:34; Isa. 30:18; 40:31). In the old covenant, the waiting of God's people concerned primarily the coming Messiah. In the new covenant God's people wait for the return of the Messiah (Rom. 8:23–25; 1 Thess. 1:10) and for glorification,[1] the final redemption of their physical bodies (Rom. 8:23).

OPPRESSION OF THE POOR. The Lord's heart for the poor and marginalized is evident in his indictment of their oppression in Judah and Ephraim (Hos. 12:7), a grievous sin condemned by the prophets and elsewhere in the Old Testament. The law made provision for the poor (Lev. 19:10, 15; 23:22), and the Wisdom Literature upholds fair treatment of the less fortunate as a mark of faithful covenant life (e.g., Prov. 14:21; 17:5). The New Testament also views mistreatment of the poor as a mark of unbelief (see James 2:1–6). The apostle Paul undertook relief efforts for poor believers (e.g., Rom. 15:25–26; 1 Cor. 16:1–3), demonstrating the biblical principle that God cares about people's physical needs as well as their spiritual needs.

Theological Soundings

GOD'S NAME. "The LORD, the God of hosts, the LORD is his memorial name" (Hos. 12:5). Long before Hosea's day, God had identified himself to Moses with the name "I AM WHO I AM" (Ex. 3:14), which is transliterated "Yahweh" and rendered in the ESV as "LORD," with small capital letters. That divine name identifies God as the creator and sustainer of all that exists. The name is also a clear reminder of God's promises to his people to be with them and help them. Jesus Christ was also called "Lord," identifying him with God. When Jesus said, "Before Abraham was, I am" (John 8:58), he was claiming identity with the God who appeared to Moses.

THE WORD OF GOD. In the Old Testament, God spoke his word through the prophets (Hos. 12:10, 13), articulating the path of obedience leading to blessing. God had also given his written Word, a process begun at Mount Sinai when he gave Moses the two tablets of stone written in his own words (Ex. 32:16). Those tablets were deposited in the ark of the covenant (Deut. 10:5) and served as the basis of the covenant relationship between God and his people.

The written Word was completed with the writings of the apostles (Rev. 22:18). After that, nothing more needed to be said, since all that was written was fulfilled in Jesus Christ (John 5:39). Jesus is the full and final Word of God (John 1:1). The covenant Lord has always been a God who speaks (Heb. 1:1–2).

Personal Implications

Take time to reflect on the implications of Hosea 11:12–12:14 for your own life today. Consider what you have learned that might lead you to trust more fully in God's Word. Make notes below on the personal implications for your walk with the Lord of the (1) *Gospel Glimpses*, (2) *Whole-Bible Connections*, (3) *Theological Soundings*, and (4) this passage as a whole.

1. Gospel Glimpses

2. Whole-Bible Connections

3. Theological Soundings

4. Hosea 11:12–12:14

▶ **As You Finish This Unit . . .**

Take a moment now to ask for the Lord's help as you continue in this study, then look back through this unit and reflect on some key things that the Lord is teaching you.

Definition

[1] **Glorification** – The work of God in believers to bring them to the ultimate and perfect stage of salvation—Christlikeness—following his justification and sanctification of them (Rom. 8:29–30). Glorification includes believers' receiving imperishable resurrection bodies at Christ's return (1 Cor. 15:42–43).

Week 10: Rejection of Hope

Hosea 13:1–16

▲

The Place of the Passage

The passage before us is grim, but there are notes of hope in Hosea's words, and glimpses of the gospel. Again we see that the idols Israel has turned to are nothing compared to God. By refusing to repent, Israel is rejecting their only hope. In the second section of Hosea 13, three figures of judgment are displayed: the incompetent king (vv. 10–11), the unborn child (vv. 13–14), and the withering wind (v. 15).

The Big Picture

In Hosea 13:1–16, God condemns Israel for her persistent worship of worthless idols.

> ## Reflection and Discussion

Read through the complete passage for this study, Hosea 13:1–16. Then review the questions below and record your notes. (For further background, see the *ESV Study Bible*, pages 1640–1641.)

1. Worship of False Gods (13:1–8)

"Those who offer human sacrifice kiss calves!" (13:2). Child sacrifice was a ritualistic component of Baal worship, and Israel's participation in it indicates how far she has fallen. Kissing was a way of paying homage (see Ps. 2:12), which is what God's people were offering to calves, as their ancestors had done before them (Exodus 32; 1 Kings 12). Why was calf worship a particular temptation for Israel?

"They sin more and more, and make for themselves metal images" (Hos. 13:2). Hosea outlines the practices involved in worshiping idols made from precious metal by skilled craftsmen. What truth is the prophet seeking to expose in this verse?

Hosea uses four similes in 13:3 to describe the effects of idol worship: mist, dew, chaff, and smoke. What do these images communicate about Israel? How is the Lord contrasted to them in verse 4?

A repeated sin pattern, one common to man in every age, is laid out in 13:6. What particular steps make up this pattern, and how can it be avoided? According to verses 7–8, where does the pattern eventually lead?

2. Rejection of Hope (13:9–16)

"I gave you a king in my anger, and I took him away in my wrath" (13:11). Israel's leadership has proven woefully ineffective, but the king's subjects carry blame as well, going back to their first king, Saul. Read about the choice of Saul as king in 1 Samuel 8:4–9. What clue is given there as to why Israel's kingship failed? What would have made a difference, and how is this difference evident in the appointment of David as king in 1 Samuel 16:1–13?

"At the right time, he does not present himself at the opening of the womb" (Hos. 13:13). Israel refuses to repent and be healed, which Hosea likens to a baby who refuses to be born. Based on the imagery in 13:12–13, what step could God's people take toward spiritual rebirth?

"Sheol" in the Old Testament is sometimes used poetically for the grave (e.g., 1 Kings 2:6; Ps. 141:7), but elsewhere it designates damnation (e.g., Ps. 49:14–15). Death is the ultimate outcome for those who refuse to repent and turn to the Lord. What is implied in the two questions asked poetically of Death and Sheol in Hosea 13:14?

Bitter consequences are spelled out graphically in 13:15–16: loss of every material thing and of life itself. When God lifts the restraints imposed by his patience and grace, there is no hope. Even when confronted with such loss, Israel remains stubborn. What truths about the nature of sin are revealed through Israel's stubbornness?

Read through the following three sections on *Gospel Glimpses*, *Whole-Bible Connections*, and *Theological Soundings*. Then take time to consider the *Personal Implications* these sections may have for you.

Gospel Glimpses

WISE SON. Ephraim was an "unwise son" (Hos. 13:13). Forsaking God, their only hope, they foolishly chose to worship gods of their own design, leading to destruction. Israel as an unwise son shows the need for a wise son, a need fulfilled in Jesus. Whereas Israel sacrificed to idols as a means of personal gain, the wise Son sacrificed himself so that others could gain. Because of sin, man is naturally foolish. No one left to himself chooses the wise path (1 Cor. 2:14), but Christ "became to us wisdom from God, righteousness, sanctification, and redemption" (1 Cor. 1:30).

DEATH DEFEATED. "O Death, where are your plagues? O Sheol, where is your sting?" (Hos. 13:14). Rejecting God results in death, the ultimate judgment, and the end was closing in on God's people in Hosea's day. But then, as now, God has triumphed over death. The plagues of Death and the sting of Sheol were defeated in the death and resurrection of Christ. The apostle Paul quotes Hosea 13:14 and exults in God's triumph over death through Christ: "The sting of death is sin, and the power of sin is the law. But thanks be to God, who gives us the victory through our Lord Jesus Christ" (1 Cor. 15:56–57).

Whole-Bible Connections

REDEMPTION. "Shall I redeem them from Death?" asks the Lord (Hos. 13:14). God has always been the redeemer of his people. Redemption was woven into the law in the institutions of property redemption (Lev. 25:23–25) and levirate marriage (Deut. 25:5–6). Redemption was also part and parcel of the sacrificial system,[1] all of which prefigured the coming of Christ. Jesus' sacrificial death is the basis of eternal redemption, the paid release from the oppression of sin. Long before the coming of Jesus, God's people knew him as redeemer (e.g., Job 19:25; Ps. 19:14; Isa. 47:4; Jer. 50:34), and the entire book of Ruth is devoted to this theme. "In him we have redemption through his blood, the forgiveness of our trespasses, according to the riches of his grace" (Eph. 1:7; see also Col. 1:14).

MAN-MADE GODS. Israel worshiped figments of their imagination put into tangible form. The so-called gods were nothing more than objects of metal crafted by human hands (Hos. 13:2). The method in which idols are created exposes the underlying reality of them: self-worship. Man-made gods have no capabilities; they cannot speak or see or hear (Ps. 115:4–7; Isa. 40:18–20)—nor can the worshipers themselves (Ps. 115:8). When Paul preached at Athens, he contrasted man-made gods with the true God (Acts 17:24–25), and elsewhere he said, "An idol has no real existence" (1 Cor. 8:4). Man-made gods take a more sophisticated form in our day, but the self-worship underlying them is the same, and for that reason, God's people are warned to flee idolatry (1 Cor. 10:14; 1 John 5:21).

Theological Soundings

SIN GUILT. "He incurred guilt through Baal and died" (Hos. 13:1). Sin brings death, both physical and spiritual, ever since the fall of Adam and Eve (Gen. 3:1–19). Every human being is guilty of sin in all areas of life (Ps. 14:1–3; Rom. 3:23) and therefore stands under just condemnation to eternal ruin, without defense or excuse (Rom. 5:12). All are under the curse brought about by the fall, and the promise of God's righteous judgment, i.e., death, is guaranteed (Rom. 6:23). This is the state from which we need to be saved and for which a Savior has been provided by God himself. Jesus Christ bore our guilt on the cross, forever satisfying the righteous wrath of God against sin. The righteousness of Christ is applied to guilty sinners who place their faith in him, and all who do so are declared "not guilty" by God (see 2 Cor. 5:21).

GOD AS HELPER. Israel rejected the Lord, who condescends to be the "helper" of his people (Hos. 13:9). God's incomparable love is demonstrated in his willingness to help sinners. In the Old Testament the Lord "rides through the heavens to your help" (Deut. 33:26), and the psalmists express their confidence in his willingness to aid (Pss. 30:10; 72:12; 118:7). In the New Testament, this aspect of the divine nature is manifested in the work of the Holy Spirit, whose helping work consists of bearing witness to Jesus (John 15:26), teaching (John 14:26), gifting (1 Cor. 12:4–11), praying for believers (Rom. 8:26–27), and providing assurance of adoption[2] (Rom. 8:16).

Personal Implications

Take time to reflect on the implications of Hosea 13:1–16 for your own life today. Consider what you have learned about the character of God. Make notes below on the personal implications for your walk with the Lord of the (1) *Gospel Glimpses*, (2) *Whole-Bible Connections*, (3) *Theological Soundings*, and (4) this passage as a whole.

1. Gospel Glimpses

2. Whole-Bible Connections

3. Theological Soundings

4. Hosea 13:1–16

As You Finish This Unit . . .

Take a moment now to ask for the Lord's help as you continue in this study, and reflect on some key things that the Lord is teaching you.

Definitions

[1] **Sacrifice** – An offering to God, often to signify forgiveness of sin. The Law of Moses gave detailed instructions regarding various kinds of sacrifices. By his death on the cross, Jesus gave himself as a sacrifice to atone for the sins of believers (Eph. 5:2; Heb. 10:12). Believers are to offer their bodies as living sacrifices to God (Rom. 12:1).

[2] **Adoption** – Legal process by which a person gives the status of a son or daughter to another person who is not his or her child by birth. The NT uses the term to describe the act by which God makes believers his children through the atoning death and resurrection of his one and only true Son, Jesus (see Romans 8; Galatians 4).

WEEK 11: FINAL APPEAL

Hosea 14:1–9

The Place of the Passage

Hosea finishes his book with a series of moving appeals to God's wayward people to return to the Lord and find healing and restoration (14:1–8). As the path back to the Lord is set forth, Hosea articulates the steps of repentance necessary for believers in every age. For emphasis, Hosea directs his final words to individual Israelites, encouraging them to pursue personal faithfulness to the covenant (v. 9).

The Big Picture

Hosea pleads with the wayward northern kingdom to return to the Lord and find healing and restoration.

Reflection and Discussion

Read through Hosea 14:1–9, the passage for this week's study. Then review the following questions, taking notes on this final section. (For further background, see the *ESV Study Bible*, pages 1641–1642.)

1. A Plea to Return to the Lord (14:1–8)

"Take with you words and return to the LORD" (14:2). Despite Israel's persistent refusal to turn back to the Lord, the invitation to return still stands, and in verses 2–3 Hosea instructs them how to approach the Lord. What components of true repentance can you identify in the "words" he directs them to pray?

"We will pay with bulls the vows of our lips" (14:2). This expression likely describes peace offerings, during which worshipers enjoyed a meal in God's presence. What would be indicated about the heart of those who could honestly include these words in a prayer of repentance?

"Assyria shall not save us; we will not ride on horses; and we will say no more, 'Our God,' to the work of our hands. In you the orphan finds mercy" (14:3). In what ways is the enslaving power of idolatry broken through repentance?

God's promise to heal their apostasy[1] will serve to deepen the intentions expressed in 14:3. God promises also to "love them freely" (v. 4). Given that God has never stopped loving his wayward people, what is meant by this divine promise?

Hosea turns again to agrarian imagery in 14:5–7 as he holds before the people what life would be like if they came back to the Lord. What do these particular images indicate? What specific reversals from earlier in the prophecy do you see here? How does this imagery serve to encourage your own repentance?

"They shall return and dwell beneath my shadow" (14:7). What does it mean to dwell beneath God's shadow? How do Psalms 17:8; 36:7; 57:1; 91:1 round out the picture?

Compare Hosea 6:1–3, which shows Israel's current state, to 14:1–8, which reveals where God wants Israel to be. Both passages articulate words of repentance. What from Hosea 14 is missing from the passage in Hosea 6?

2. An Apt Conclusion (14:9)

Those who are wise and discerning will "understand these things" and "know" them experientially. Hosea's final words stand in direct contrast to Israel's failure to know, emphasized throughout the book (2:8; 5:4; 8:1–3; 11:3). According to Deuteronomy 4:5–6; Job 28:28; Psalm 111:10; and Proverbs 1:7; 9:10, what is the nature of the wisdom required to know the Lord?

"The ways of the LORD are right, and the upright walk in them, but transgressors stumble in them" (Hos. 14:9). In what way does rejecting God cause the rebellious to stumble? The full picture comes in the New Testament: how do Luke 2:34 and 2 Corinthians 2:15–16 complete our understanding? How does one "walk" in God's ways?

Read through the following three sections on *Gospel Glimpses*, *Whole-Bible Connections*, and *Theological Soundings*. Then take time to consider the *Personal Implications* these sections may have for you.

Gospel Glimpses

APOSTASY HEALED. "I will heal their apostasy" (Hos. 14:4). Sin as sickness, an incurable disease (Jer. 17:9), is evident throughout Israel's history. Sin's fatal prognosis shows the need for divine healing. God's healing work in the Old Testament (Ex. 15:26; 23:25; Num. 21:6–9) foreshadows the work of Christ (John 3:14–15). The remedy has been provided in Christ, who came to heal (Matt. 9:12). The promise for the repentant in Hosea 14 foreshadows the coming of Christ, who came so that all might be healed (Rev. 22:2).

LOVE FREELY GIVEN. "I will love them freely" (Hos. 14:4). The magnitude of God's grace is seen in his ongoing love in the face of rejection. Despite Israel's sin, he has never stopped loving them; if they would only repent, his love would flow out in blessings unhindered by the prospect of coming judgment. His offer of full and free love to Israel is seen most fully in the sending of his Son in order to restore to himself those alienated by sin (John 3:16; Rom. 5:8; 1 John 4:9–10).

Whole-Bible Connections

RENEWAL. If Israel would return to the Lord, God would "heal their apostasy" (Hos. 14:4). Israel would "blossom like the lily" (v. 5) and "flourish like the grain" (v. 7). Pictured here is a process of renewal whereby what has been damaged by sin is restored to wholeness. Moses held out the same promise when the covenant was renewed in Moab (see Deut. 30:1–3). Divine renewal has been unfolding since man's fall into sin (Ps. 103:5), and one day all of creation will be fully restored (Rev. 21:5). Through Christ, all that is perishable will be raised and transformed into a glorious new reality (Rom. 8:21; 1 Cor. 15:42–43).

WISDOM. Hosea ends his prophecy with an appeal to wisdom. The wise "understand" the ways of God, and the "discerning" know them experientially (Hos. 14:9). Wisdom is defined as "the fear of the LORD" (Ps. 111:10; Prov. 1:7; 9:10), which involves living in humble reliance on God and in faithful obedience to his ways within the covenant community. Wisdom resides in the character of God and was woven into the fabric of creation (Prov. 8:22–31). Due to sin, mankind is foolish rather than wise, but Christ became wisdom on behalf of God's people (1 Cor. 1:24, 30). In him are "all the treasures of wisdom and knowledge" (Col. 2:3). Those united to him are enabled to live wisely in an evil age, thus demonstrating the genuineness of their faith (James 3:13–18).

> ### Theological Soundings

REPENTANCE. "Return, O Israel, to the LORD your God" (Hos. 14:1). Israel's returning to God will involve a complete change of heart and mind toward God, exhibited not only in the words they say but also in how they think and act. Those who truly repent will acknowledge the guilt of their sin and express a desire for its removal, and their confession will be accompanied by a renewed desire for fellowship with God and participation in covenant obedience (v. 2). As repentance is lived out, wrong thinking is replaced by right understanding of God and the world at large (v. 3). In both Testaments it is clear that our ability to repent is a gift from God. He allures his wayward people back to himself (Hos. 2:14; Rom. 2:4) and disciplines them to that end (Hos. 10:10; Heb. 12:3–6). Although God stirs repentance in his people, they are responsible to respond from the heart and forsake their sin (1 John 1:8–10). Nevertheless, even our repentance is tainted by sin. Therefore, our hope lies not in perfecting our repentance but in the One who procured it for us (see Jude 24).

JUDGMENT. The book of Hosea ends on a somber note: those who refuse to walk in God's ways will "stumble in them" (14:9). Ultimately, God cannot be avoided. Those who embrace him, the "wise" and "discerning," will "know" his ways and experience blessing, but those who reject him will find increasing frustration and futility and, finally, eternal destruction (Prov. 10:29). As foretold by Isaiah, Jesus Christ is the ultimate line of division (Isa. 8:13–15), the one "appointed for the fall and rising of many in Israel, and for a sign that is opposed, . . . so that thoughts from many hearts may be revealed" (Luke 2:34–35). "The one who falls on this stone will be broken to pieces" (Matt. 21:44), but to those who turn to him in faith, he is a "cornerstone chosen and precious, and whoever believes in him will not be put to shame" (1 Pet. 2:6).

Personal Implications

Take time to reflect on the implications of Hosea 14:1–9 for your own life today. Consider what you have learned that might lead you to praise God, repent of sin, and walk in his abiding love. Make notes below on the personal implications for your walk with the Lord of the (1) *Gospel Glimpses*, (2) *Whole-Bible Connections*, (3) *Theological Soundings*, and (4) this passage as a whole.

1. Gospel Glimpses

2. Whole-Bible Connections

3. Theological Soundings

4. Hosea 14:1–9

As You Finish This Unit . . .

Take a moment now to ask for the Lord's blessing as you continue in this study. Look back through this unit to reflect on some key things that the Lord may be teaching you.

Definition

[1] **Apostasy** – Abandonment or renunciation of faith.

WEEK 12: SUMMARY AND CONCLUSION

▲

We conclude our study by summarizing the big picture of God's message through Hosea as a whole. Then we will consider several questions in order to reflect on various Gospel Glimpses, Whole-Bible Connections, and Theological Soundings throughout the entire book.

The Big Picture of Hosea

Hosea prophesied as Assyrian dominance was spreading across the entire ancient Near East, posing a significant threat to God's people. This threat hanging over Israel, most imminently the northern kingdom—called "Ephraim" by Hosea—coincided with political upheaval and instability in Israel itself and a loss of trust in God.

Hosea's major concerns were Israel's attempts to form alliances with foreign powers and the worship of Baal, a weather god who supposedly had control over agriculture and fertility. Aspects of Baal worship included drunkenness, sexual perversion, and human sacrifice, activities God's people were practicing.

By recalling incidents from Israel's past, Hosea seeks to remind the people that they belong to the Lord. Once the Lord's delightful bride, Israel has betrayed that intimate and privileged union, committing acts of spiritual adultery. Because Israel refuses to repent, judgment is coming in the form of what the people dreaded most—exile from the land. But punishment is not ultimately what the Lord wants for his people; he desires them to return to him and be renewed in covenant blessings.

In the first major section of the book (1:1–3:5), Hosea draws from his troubled marriage to Gomer, her unfaithfulness, and their eventual restoration as a parable for the Lord's relationship to Israel. In the rest of the book (4:1–14:9), Hosea exposes Israel's unfaithfulness to the Lord, urges repentance, and sets forth God's powerful and passionate commitment to his people in spite of their unfaithfulness.

Gospel Glimpses

Israel's apostasy and God's pending judgment pervade Hosea's prophecy, yet what the book presents is ultimately a love story. God will not forsake his people even though they have rejected him, and in his love he will go to great lengths to win back their hearts. Using the language of a lover, Hosea reveals God's heart as that of a husband who allures and speaks tenderly (2:14, 16), yet who experiences the grief of a betrayed lover (6:4; 11:8). Such divine love in the face of blatant apostasy foreshadows the love of Jesus, who came to serve those who would reject him. God's promise to heal the apostasy of his people and love them freely (14:4) points to the finished work of Christ—his death and resurrection—through which eternal healing and love are found.

How has Hosea clarified your understanding of the gospel?

What passages or themes in Hosea have strengthened your grasp of God's grace to us through Jesus?

Whole-Bible Connections

Hosea shows us the nature of the relationship God desires with his people. From the call of the patriarchs, which Hosea recalls (12:3–6), to the establishment of the Mosaic covenant, the Lord had provided for relational intimacy and had made his loving intentions known. Hosea frequently refers to the Pentateuch, the foundation of Israel's relationship to God. Israel repeatedly rejected this privileged calling, and by Hosea's day the time for judgment had come. Yet God's love for his people is such that his judgments ultimately work restoration rather than destruction. The isolation of the exile that soon followed would be a means to restoration (1:6–7; 2:14–23; 3:1–3; 5:6–6:3; 11:8–11; 12:9). For Ephraim to return to the Lord, the people must return to the house of David (3:5), and from the house of David the ultimate king for God's people would come. Sin brought judgment, but through it God would work a glorious future for his people.

How has this study of Hosea enriched your understanding of the overall thread of redemptive history?

What aspects of Hosea's prophecy enable you to better understand the Bible as a unified whole?

What connections between Hosea and the New Testament were new to you?

> ## Theological Soundings

By undertaking this study of Hosea, we see that theology (what we believe about God) is important, playing a vital role in living the Christian life. In Hosea, particular attributes of God are emphasized, most especially his love and justice. Other attributes revealed are his omniscience, sovereignty, and mercy. In contrast, the nature of sin is laid bare, especially the sin of idolatry. Sin blinds, enslaves, twists the mind, and warps one's view of reality. The nature of man's depravity, clearly seen in Hosea, demonstrates that divine rescue is needed—a Savior who can do what man in his fallen state cannot do.

Has your view of sin changed while studying Hosea—sin in general and your own in particular?

Through studying Hosea, what have you learned about the nature of idolatry?

How has your understanding of God changed throughout this study?

In what particular ways does Hosea point forward to Jesus and what he accomplished through his life, death, and resurrection?

Personal Implications

What in your thinking and your day-to-day life is already changing as a result of studying Hosea?

How has studying Hosea deepened your dependence on Christ?

As You Finish Studying Hosea . . .

The book of Hosea consists primarily of judgment oracles and allusions to aspects of life in ancient Israel, many of which are difficult to grasp, but the riches contained within it are well worth the labor. We hope that all you have learned will prove to be life changing. We encourage you to study the Word of God on a week-by-week basis. To continue your study of the Bible, please consider other books in the *Knowing the Bible* series, which can be found at www.knowingthebibleseries.org.

Lastly, take a moment to look back through this study. Review the notes you have written and the things you have highlighted or underlined. Reflect again on the key themes that the Lord has been teaching you about himself and about his Word.

Experience the *Grace* of God in the *Word* of God, Book by Book

KNOWING THE BIBLE STUDY GUIDE SERIES

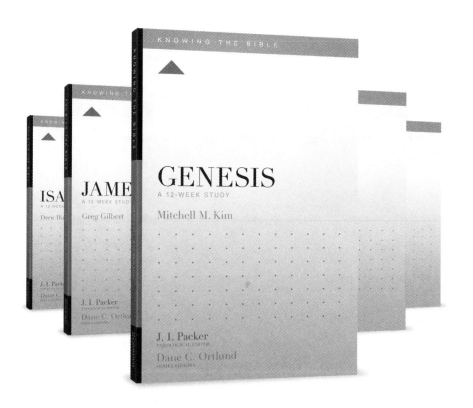

· · · · · · · · · ·CURRENT VOLUMES · · · · · · · · ·

Genesis	Proverbs	Mark	Galatians
Exodus	Ecclesiastes	Luke	Ephesians
Leviticus	Isaiah	John	Philippians
Joshua	Jeremiah	Acts	Colossians and Philemon
Ruth and Esther	Daniel	Romans	Hebrews
Ezra and Nehemiah	Hosea	1 Corinthians	James
Psalms	Matthew	2 Corinthians	Revelation

crossway.org